The Fast Track to Your Ideal Job

When job finding is easy, your ideal job is within reach

SCOTT F. LANGMACK

The Fast Track to Your Ideal Job

ISBN: 0615724779
ISBN-13: 9780615724775

For Diane Howell

The Fast Track to Your Ideal Job

Preface

This book will help you get a great job. Although many believe that setting a timeframe for finding a job is unrealistic, the steps outlined within these pages will show you that it is possible to find the job you always wanted without spending much time. Although there are numerous job-finding books in the market, this one is different and is proven to work. It will show you that making changes and attaining career success is easy. So, have fun reading and get ready for great things.

The process of invention can be one of the most rewarding experiences in your work life. Thus, why not start thinking of yourself as an invention in progress—an invention designed to add value to others by doing something you love. All you need to do is open your eyes and the plan for this invention will be revealed to you within the pages of this book. Most importantly, never settle for less than you know you deserve.

I have been coaching people on job finding and careers for some twenty years and have seen the job market from many perspectives—as an interviewer, hiring manager, job search coach, job industry technology entrepreneur, just to name a few. I have run large business groups in companies such as Microsoft and Wilson Sporting Goods, led global marketing for Pepsi-Cola, and I've been involved with tech start-ups backed by top venture capital firms, such as Kleiner Perkins Caufield and Byers and Benchmark Capital. I am currently the CEO of BlueChipExec.com—a web company that automates the key principles outlined in this book.

My journey that has led me to this point, like most people's stories, has several seminal moments that represent my own process of self-invention and reinvention.

I had an unconventional, yet terrific childhood, which included numerous moves—from California, to Arizona, to Maryland, to England, to Norway, and back to California. This has provided many challenges, as I had to quickly adapt to new surroundings, make new friends, and leave the old life behind, but has also provided plenty of vivid memories of sledding in Maryland, rowing a boat across a fjord in Norway, playing soccer in boarding school in England, and camping with Boy Scouts with my dad as Scoutmaster.

My life changed dramatically when I was eleven years old, as my dad moved across the country, *without us*. From then on, I would see him for no more than a weekend or two a year. My dad was a dreamer, and like many dreamers, he lacked sound business sense. In hindsight, he had a knack for selecting the worst business partners possible. As a result, from my teen years onward he was always broke, but as a child I never lost hope that things would change and I would go on to get a new drum set, a grand ski vacation, or get a new motorcycle for my next birthday or as a Christmas present.

The birthdays and Christmases came and went, and not only did the presents not arrive, but my dad was so embarrassed to have failed to fulfill his promises, that he would often not even call. It was quite an empty feeling, and although my mom was a star and did everything she could, I eventually realized that I could no longer rely on my father. I woke up the morning after my thirteenth birthday with a new perspective. I knew deep down that anything I was "expecting" to get in my life I would have to earn for myself. This new perspective allowed me to pass through the rest of my adolescence without being angry at my dad, as I understood that he meant well, and he just wasn't able to find a way to make money without getting an actual job.

Looking back, this was the most influential time in my life, as it helped me understand the importance of personal responsibility. The benefit of seeing the world this way was simple—I realized that, in order to get what I wanted in life, I needed to create and implement a plan that could lead to success. However, the flipside of this approach is fear. Once you live through being broke—the kind of broke where you can't pay the rent, your belongings are repossessed, and you can't repair the car—you don't want to be in that place again.

My next pivotal point in life that provided me with yet another essential perspective came when I was a sophomore in college and started to consider my future. I decided that, since I was going to work for the rest of my life, it would be far better to work in great jobs than lousy ones. It wasn't hard for me to envision that a great job would be a combination of something that I would enjoy doing that also paid well. I pursued that objective by getting an MBA at the University of Southern California, and getting a foothold was easier from that point on. I know now that the advanced degree is a shortcut, but you don't need one to get your career on the fast track.

My own experience in job finding throughout the years included all the ups and downs that most people experience. Initially, I had no idea whatsoever on how to get a job, and over time I let the coincidental opportunities that presented themselves direct my interest. Even so, there were jobs that I wanted badly and didn't get. In some cases, I was so unprepared that I shot myself in the foot. There were interviews where I had no idea what I was doing or saying, and I mostly looked for an exit door. Still, over time, I had just enough luck and confidence to get into some great roles and I've had a lot of fun working in those positions.

The experiences I went through over the years gave me an idea for this book and a website, as I felt that I could help other job seekers find their ideal jobs. In 2010, I realized that the years most affected by the recession have left many without jobs and no idea how to get one. As I pondered on this issue, I discovered a fundamental problem: The most stable employees were often the least informed and confident in their approach to finding a job. These people just had very little experience in the job search process, and most were unsure of how or where to look for a plan.

Although most of us have looked for and found several jobs over the years, and everyone seems to have an opinion on how to best approach job search, I could not find a book or a website that provided a clear answer to the questions: What is the ideal job search plan? What is the most efficient and effective way for people to go about a job search? How can people conduct a job search that is energizing and void of the drudgery so common in a job search?

I was meeting with people because I had a background in technology solutions, having started a company that integrated the elements of career sites, HR departments, hiring managers, recruiting firms, and job seekers. In this process I worked closely for several years with heads of HR from top companies, which helped me understand the dizzying amount of technology solutions they are presented with. Mostly, they wrestle with an evolving state of the job posting and job application management, and they all seem to be trying to sort out how to get more candidates from internal referrals. I also worked with many executive search consultants, head hunters as they are affectionately called, which gave me an insider's understanding about how their industry works. And since I was running a jobs tech company in Silicon Valley, I studied the competitive environment of job web sites.

It was during dozens and dozens of sessions with job seekers that I realized the conventional wisdom for job hunting, many of the guides on job hunting, and most people's advice were wrong. Besides lacking a clear direction, people were being swayed by a job posting industry that had lost all relevance, and most people simply were not aware of how futile most of their efforts were.

Knowing how the primary elements of the job industry worked made it easy for me to coach others through the job search process. Within a few months, I started receiving the letters of success and joy, and it occurred to me that the coaching I was providing was essentially allowing people to master the techniques that have been proven over time. I could finally answer the question, "What is the ideal job search?" I knew how to make this process energizing and easy, instead of depressing and hard. The necessity of providing the right blend of technology, planning and process became apparent.

So I wrote this book and created BlueChipExec.com to help both employed and unemployed people get their ideal jobs. The logic behind my plan is simple: If you can learn how to make the job-searching process easy, why settle? Sadly, many people do settle, no matter how unhappy they are with their current situation. According to the research recently conducted by Right Management,[1] over eighty percent of employed people say that they plan to change jobs in the next year! Unfortunately, most of the survey respondents will never even attempt to look for another job, let alone get one, as they will fear change. The painful truth is that staying in a job that you are not excited about is far more risky, as you can't do your best work if you are in a job that you don't like. As is often the case in human history, fear causes us to avoid the decisions that may be in our best interests.

Conventional wisdom suggests that it should take five to nine months to get executive level jobs, and less than that for a manager and individual contributor jobs. I strongly disagree with these generic timeframes and will show you that, if you follow the advice presented in this book, you will get more done in the next six weeks than most people do in a year of job searching. I will also

1 2012 research conducted by Right Management Group, a division of Manpower, indicated that of over 1000 people surveyed, more than 86% said that "they plan to get a different job next year."

show you how those six weeks will require less work and energy than the typical job search.

I hope that you are energized and motivated to follow the key steps in the book—they go beyond the job search and will help you continue on the path of success and fulfillment through your entire professional life. Before you start reading, all I will ask of you is to be open-minded and optimistic. Most importantly, please never settle.

Prologue

The past often holds important lessons that can foretell the future, yet as the human race hurls itself relentlessly forward, few seek insight by looking back. For a moment, picture the world before everything was digitized. This is a span of thousands of years in which the role of the community was the basis for safety, trust, and productivity. Communities defined the social construct, and the roles that people assumed through an interdependence of skills required for clothing, food, and shelter.

The community was simply a fabric of interwoven individuals, linked in a way that created both trust and familiarity. People cared for each other, grew together, and raised each other's children, truly believing that "it takes a village...." They supported the local vendors, warned each other of suspicious events, and gave a helping hand when a fellow community member fell upon hard times. This was a time accidentally focused on the relationships that helped careers, and where advice and direction was provided at every turn to enable young people to find their best path.

This world was one of shared ideas and unexpected friendships. People naturally made introductions, suggestions, endorsements, and created job opportunities for someone they liked. More experienced community members would take on apprentices, or protégés, and guide them in mastering skills for a certain profession. As societies were so closely knit and bad reputation was difficult to hide from, people worked hard to protect their integrity. The bond of the human social animal with the choices involved in finding work was inseparable.

Now, imagine a different world where digitization, automation, computerization, information overload, and global connectivity prevail. People no longer bump into each other on the street, as they don't need to leave the safety of their homes and their electronic devices very often. Everything is delivered to their doorstep and their lives have become streamlined and efficient. People no longer meet face to face; they rarely speak on the phone and instead send emails and text messages. People no longer gather in larger groups to meet new people, but instead connect to friends or even people they will never meet on social networking sites. People no longer reach out to acquaintances to catch up over a coffee, as all that's required now is to verify a LinkedIn request. As computerization has grown, people become less human.

In this world, the reciprocal role of mentoring has suffered, as the understanding of the necessity to seek and provide advice has withered. The willingness to reach up to influential people or to help those just starting in a job has faded. The result is a population that is stymied and confused. Many try to use digitization to help them with their careers, but most come up empty handed. Despite this, digitization has expanded the process of job finding at exponential rates; it has enabled thousands of people to apply for the same jobs simultaneously, allowing prospective employers to process the applications at ever increasing rates. Buried in technology overload, the digital work has no end, and for the job seekers, very few beginnings.

Finding a job through the Internet is one of the least-effective methods in this digital world. But in a computer-driven world with thousands of solutions, the irony is that the ineffective computer is still perceived to be the best way to find a job. Technology is sadly making us less human, stripping us of the essential ingredients that have been the engine of mankind since the beginning of time.

The answer may just lie in the understanding that, although the computer can be a useful job searching tool, there is no computer as powerful as the human mind when it comes to job finding.

SECTION I

Get Set

Before embarking on your job search, you should first learn a bit about the job search industry, and get familiar with the rules that will make the job finding easy.

CHAPTER 1

The Ideal Job Is Easy to Find

Consider the following question—"How would you live your life if finding a new job was easy?" For most people, this may be more challenging than it seems at first, as they have never considered this question. Still, it is important to carefully consider the answer, as it reflects our views of employment, and how hard most of us hold onto whatever job we are in. But before we look into the answers, let's raise the stakes . . . Spend some time considering how you would live your life if it was easy to find your *ideal* job.

If finding an ideal job was easy, it is highly likely that you would do just that. For people who are unemployed, assuming that they want to be productive and work, it's an obvious "yes." They need to look for a job anyway, so aiming for an ideal job does not require a significant change in their objectives. However, for an employed person, the opportunity to easily find an ideal job creates a degree of freedom and flexibility that may just change the way you see work altogether. If given a chance to find an ideal job, instead of spending your energy trying to sort out ways to tolerate a job that makes you crazy, you would enthusiastically seek to learn about what that ideal job could be.

You might explore different industries, as the sector you choose to work in can make a big difference in the levels of your job satisfaction. Each industry implies a certain pace, requires a certain driving force, provides a certain culture, and follows a series of best practices. You will most likely find that one industry fits with your personal interests and work style better than another.

Once you have identified your preferred industry, you might explore different roles, such as marketing, sales, or partnership management, among others. Different roles require markedly different skills, and your ideal job would utilize your current skills, providing opportunities to perform tasks you enjoy the most, as well as allow you to acquire new skills and progress in your career path in your chosen industry.

You might also explore different companies within an industry, as different companies have different approaches to employees, teamwork, management, independence, structure, autonomy, and productivity.

You would keep narrowing down your selection until you have a clear understanding of the role, the company, and the industry that you wish to work in. You would keep researching until you found the job that would make you excited to get up in the morning and face every working day with a smile and optimism. You would find a role that would make you lose yourself in your work and lose track of time. You would identify a company where you would feel respected and enjoy interacting with the people around you. Once you've found that job, you would stay until something changed and it was time to move on.

If you had an ideal job, you would find a sense of self-determination and control that would enable you to work at a level that was immensely productive and deeply satisfying. In that capacity, you would likely be in demand, and your compensation would continually grow. You would find peace and confidence about yourself and your future, which is a magical place to be in.

Conventional wisdom suggests that most people think that finding a job is very hard—so hard that they dread the idea of even starting the process. Some find the idea so challenging that they choose to stay in jobs they hate, because actively making the changes is just too repugnant. Job search is perceived as so hard that even unemployed and those in desperate need of a job have a hard time committing to the process of job hunting.

Yet, the truth is that job finding can be easy and the secret to making it effortless lies in three areas:

1. You need to distinguish between what works and what doesn't, and focus on the former
2. You need to have some targeted computer assistance to take the hard work off your shoulders
3. You need to make the decision to connect with people and not allow baseless fears to get in the way of pursuing your career goals

You may think that this seems too simple to be effective, yet in my experience advising job seekers, I have found that very few people plan their time effectively. In fact, I often see that, as they continue seeking a job, they tend to fall into the worst possible scenario. Here is the typical pattern:

- 8:30 a.m.—get up, have a leisurely breakfast, read the paper
- 9:45—go for a walk or a run (exercise feels good and gets the body moving)
- 11:30—sit down with a cup of coffee at the computer and send some emails
- 11:50—browse through different jobs posted through various services
- 12:30 p.m.—start working on an application for a job posting that looks good
- 12:45—realize that you are hungry, so you break from the awful application process and prepare some lunch
- 1:30—back to completing the job application

- 2:30—no more job postings look interesting, so spend time reading news and updating Facebook
- 3:00—spouse calls, needs help picking up kids and getting them to their next appointment, so all is lost until 4:30
- 4:30—make a phone call to a contact, get no answer
- 5:15—have this conversation with spouse: "I worked all day on the job search; there is just nothing out there! I applied for more jobs, looked through hundreds of job postings, hunted on the Internet for more leads and still got nothing."

For people in this cycle, the above routine repeats, day after day, week after week, and the job seeker is in a mind-twisting quagmire of feeling the urgency to find a job, yet not getting much done. The job seeker avoids the hard work, all the while trying to justify the lack of results to him/herself and his/her spouse. In this high-pressure state of mind, the search becomes a pointless chore, something that has no clear end in sight and no obvious reward. The lack of plan and a clear objective starts to affect the ego. As the number of résumés and applications that receive no responses grows, serious doubt in one's self-worth starts to emerge. The process of sharing your greatest skills, offering yourself and your commitment, and asking for consideration is hard for even the most confident individuals. Yet, when it fails to generate any positive results, there is a risk that we would suffer a blow to our self-worth.

With so many blows over so much time, job seekers often fall into a state of mild depression. This is one of the most negative forces job seekers face.

While the example above may not describe all scenarios, it gives you an idea of the general trend. There are many different levels of intensity with which people approach a job search; some work diligently, every day, performing the same activities, but with increasing intensity. The challenge is that pursuing this "standard" approach to job hunting is inefficient, ineffective and very hard. This is the destructive outcome of an industry that is not designed to help the job seekers, but rather serve as a vehicle for hiring companies to simplify their own effort of obtaining a vast pool of candidates to choose from.

What a rough predicament to be in! This is the status of many people at all levels—from a college student looking for a first job to a senior executive seeking a career change. The importance of validation, acceptance, and a chance cannot be underestimated, yet little of this is happening if we choose to follow the "standard" approach to job search.

Knowing the difference between an effective and ineffective job search is the first step out of this downward spiral into self-doubt. The irony is that the most effective and the most efficient job search is in fact very easy and can be energizing.

This brings me to the next point, and I'm going to emphasize it, as it will be a recurring theme in this book—*Jobs come from people, not computers.* Don't throw out your computer after reading this, as you'll need it to make the most effective search easy. Still, you must understand that there is a wrong kind of computer application/ site, and a right kind. The wrong kind of site presents you with work opportunities and expects your input on a regular basis—i.e. answering job postings, filling the application forms, doing various tests, etc. The right kind of computer applications/sites will do the computer work for you. Makes sense, right? Computers talk to computers, so you might as well have your computer do that talking for you. Automation is leverage, and the right automation can make a big difference.

I have noted above that the third key to job search success is connecting with people and getting over the fears that stop all of us from taking the simplest steps to success. I hesitate to use the word "networking," as it has rather negative connotations. In my view, there are two different types of networking—one is painful and hard, and one is easy and fun.

When making new connections with the intention of finding a job, it is hard to convince a person you just met to help you in some meaningful way. I call this "cold networking," as it reminds me of the "cold calling" often utilized in sales. Although I do not favor this approach, to those that use it I would note that it requires a predetermined aptitude. People who are good at cold networking do it so naturally and effortlessly that they are probably not reading this book. The other ninety-six percent of us find cold networking an extremely hard hill to climb and would rather stick pins in our eyes than go to conventions and try to meet people who could potentially help us with our careers.

Since cold networking is hard and ineffective, it will come as no surprise that it is not part of a smart job search plan I will present here.

The opposite of cold networking is "warm networking," which is simply the process of meeting with people with whom you have some kind of personal connection. This is the most powerful way to connect and a strange, almost odd quality of being human. When you have known someone in the past, or you know someone who knows that person, arranging a meeting and developing subsequent interaction is easy. Why? Because people are social animals. Personal connections are the fabric of what makes the world go around. Inherent in social connections is the understanding of respect and generosity.

When you have some personal connection with a person, meeting and starting a conversation is as easy as cold networking is hard. If you understand that connecting *with right people for right reasons* is being fundamental to careers, and if you know how to do this well, job search is easier and more effective. This book will take you through the core theories so you too will arrive at that conclusion.

Ethics (don't skip this section)

Ethics tends to be a topic that is either studied in detail as a part of college curriculum, or not addressed at all. How you are perceived by others, and specifically how ethical you are perceived to be, will have an enormous impact on your job search and your career. Although I refer to different elements of ethical standards throughout the book, it is worth summarizing the following overarching components:

1. Treat everyone equally and in line with how you would like to be treated. Your conduct should reflect a high level of respect, regardless of the person's position or station in life. In business, people are often highly respectful of those who are more senior, and yet dismissive of more junior colleagues. While this may be a subconscious pattern, it will be seen by those with excellent character as unacceptable. Moreover, if you treat someone badly, it is likely that you will develop a bad reputation, as you never know who that person knows. So, for practical purposes, it makes sense to work hard to brighten the day for everyone you come across. Not to mention that you'll feel better about yourself for doing so.

2. Never speak badly of anyone during your interview process. This is a great habit to hold onto in general, of course, but particularly during the job search. It is a sign of poor taste to speak negatively about your company or former supervisors. This is always seen as a negative reflection on you, not them. There are two dimensions to this–first, the person you are interviewing will wonder if you are going to say negative things about them next, and second, people like to hire positive people, and if somebody is negative in an interview, the expectation is that they will be even more so when on the job.

3. Be honest about your past. In both your résumé and your descriptions of your prior work and achievements, it is important to be as honest as you can be. People often lie in order to appear more successful or to cover up something that they do not want to be revealed. The problem is that

if/when a lie is discovered, it leads to a cascading set of problems. First, you will automatically be eliminated from consideration, but more importantly, if you were referred by a friend for the position, you now also reflect very poorly on your friend. Sometimes the company will even get back to the referrer with the report of the problem and, as you can imagine, that is an unacceptable violation of the trust that person placed in you.

4. Exercise humility in reference to prior accomplishments. One of the great challenges in the job search process is to describe your accomplishments with some degree of humility. One technique is to give credit to the team you worked with, citing that you contributed in certain areas, as did others on the team, thus jointly working towards realizing the set goals. This achieves two important aims. First, you are seen as more humble, more realistic, and consequently more likable. Even though you are in job search mode, nobody likes a bragger. Second, companies are simply groups of many teams trying to get things done together. Many people struggle to work well in teams, and those who thrive when working with teams are tremendously valuable.

Change and You

One of the more interesting companies in business is the consulting firm McKinsey & Co., as they apply a fundamental principle in their approach to securing clients, whereby they first gain an agreement with their clients on these two issues:

1. You have a real problem that needs to be solved
2. The path you are on will not solve it

Once they get the client to agree to the above, they simply say, "Good thing that we are here." From there, they progress to reviewing all the successes they have had in helping companies create new strategies, develop a new plan, and sometimes even help with the execution. When dealing with large corporations, the stakes are high, and they charge accordingly.

This format is a way to convince the most stubborn CEOs to understand and accept that they *must* change. It demonstrates what is involved in the process of accepting the fact that change is required. It demonstrates that none of us has all the answers and sometimes we need guidance. Some also have difficulty accepting a change, as they cannot envisage how it would affect them.

I share this story because, since you are reading this book, I will assume that you are not in your ideal job. You are likely not waking up every morning excited to go to work. You are probably not thrilled with your productivity and accomplishment at the end of each day. You are not going to bed each night filled with the sense of potential and opportunity.

So let me be so bold as to say that you have a problem.

For people who are trying to improve their own job search or career strategy, I will also say that what you are doing now will not solve your problem. So, rather than accepting the status quo, you should dig into this book's approach and get your new path rolling.

The only question is whether you, like the top corporate CEOs, accept the idea that you need to change. If you read this book, put it down, and go back to doing what you were previously doing, your life will not change.

Albert Einstein left us with many great advancements in science, but one of my favorite Einstein legacies is this quote: "Doing the same thing over and over again and expecting a different result is the definition of insanity."

When changing your job is done right, it is easy. Get ready to change.

Key Takeaways:

- People get jobs from other people, not computers
- Most people do not approach the job search in the right way
- The computer is useful for specific tasks only (details in subsequent chapters)
- The most effective job search techniques are the easiest, so commit to making the change for the better

CHAPTER 2

The Most Important Lesson

One of the most profound and poorly understood dimensions of business, careers, and job finding is a little insight into the human soul. When I first discovered this insight a few years ago, I realized that, had I known about it before, my own career probably would have taken different paths. After talking to many people and sharing this insight, I was rather surprised that only a few understood this principle. Moreover, the people who did understand it have never interviewed for a job.

The insight has three parts:

1. <u>No one can be successful alone.</u> Everything that the world has to offer you is going to come with and through people. Someone has to hire you, someone has to promote you, and if you have your own business, someone has to buy your products or request your services. Obvious? Well, perhaps, but let me contrast it with a common theme that I hear: "I'm going to work very hard and demonstrate such excellent results that I will be recognized and rewarded." Okay, this is all well and good, but in a world that still requires someone to recognize your good work, you need to understand how people play a role in your life and career. Sadly, very often the people doing the excellent

work are NOT getting the recognition because of the skillful manipulations of others around them.

2. Successful people want to help others. Working hard and succeeding puts people into a mindset of generosity and a desire to help others. And why not? Giving feels good. If you can give just by talking and sharing ideas, you get to feel good with very little personal cost. It is easy for successful people to feel good, to give, and to help others, so many of them do. If giving felt bad, and if helping others was a painful burden, people wouldn't give or get help very often. From a broader perspective, how would the world function if the primary impulse was to *not* help others? Successful individuals also know that people are essential to jobs and careers, providing connections, mentors, and inspiration. People are sources of ideas, energy, and creativity. When two people get together, the combined power of their minds and ideas is far greater than that of one alone. This is one of the most energizing parts of life. Look for it, and rely on it in your job search process.

3. If you ask a successful person to meet about your career, they are flattered. This is the most earth-shattering and misunderstood dynamic in the world. Okay, this is a rash statement, but the possibilities behind this principle are hard to comprehend. It does have one caveat, though—you need to have some kind of personal connection to the person you are requesting help from. That person could be someone you meet regularly, such as a next-door neighbor, or knew years ago, such as your soccer coach when you were eight years old. It could even be your close friend's boss or your mom's boss. The desire for generosity and connecting when there is a personal connection is mystically strong. When that connection is established, a very human thing happens to the person being asked. They are flattered that, of all the people in the world, you decided to reach out

to them for advice. Your request says, "I admire you—your successes, accomplishments, choices, and your character. You are someone worthy of looking up to." This most human of qualities strips the grand title right off the receiver, as CEOs of Fortune 100 companies are people too, with feelings *and* egos. And I think you can see the potential. This combination—successful people wanting to help others, as well as being flattered by the request—provides the asker with resources, good intentions, creative brainwaves, ideas, and energy that can have more effect in one meeting than five years of online job applications.

Before moving on, stop and think about these three rules, and make sure that you permanently lock this concept into your mind. Make it part of how you see people and perceive the world. Make it part of what you are and how you strive to live your life. The benefits are immeasurable, and it's easy.

Successful people want to help
They are flattered when you ask[2]

The psychological depth of how and why this works is worthy of a book unto its own. Let's look at one key dimension.

The Young Person Reaching Out to a Senior Executive

When a twenty-something person asks a senior executive in his/her forties or early fifties for a meeting about career advice, the executive is keenly aware that most of us should get our footing in the business in our twenties. This is the time when we begin to shape

2 From *Never Eat Alone*, by Keith Ferrazzi

our expertise, and, if we focused well and worked hard, as we enter our thirties, we are becoming experts in our chosen field. At that point, we are ready to reap the benefits of the 10,000 hours of practice in a field, which is—according to some career authors—the key to attaining expertise.

Yet, in my view, you are still at the beginning. This period in your professional life is similar to the adolescence of business. You know enough to think that you know it all, but you have not yet learned the bigger lessons that will take you to higher leadership positions. The senior executive sees this clearly, and since he/she sees the asker as a "tenderfoot," the executive naturally has compassion and gentleness in mind.

However, another factor also plays a role here—the element of age. Youth has energy and strength in its optimism, obliviousness, and dreams. Older people are energized and inspired by youth. When an older person meets with a young person, they are thrown back to a time when they were young. That youthful view, that youthful magic, is an elixir. So, when we ask someone senior for help, we add the elixir of youth to the magic of the desire to help and the element of being flattered.

Are you seeing the power now? I use the word "power" purposefully. You have the power. The power to flatter. The power to make someone feel good through giving. The power to make someone feel good just by exchanging your youthful exuberance with them. It's real, and the degree to which you embody this and live it will affect your level of success in life dramatically and significantly.

I find that even when people intellectually understand that successful people want to help, they still have a hard time asking for it. Why? After working with hundreds of people, I have discovered that there are so many reasons, or fears, that people come up with as excuses for not seeking help. I refer to this dynamic as Networking Paralysis.

Networking Paralysis

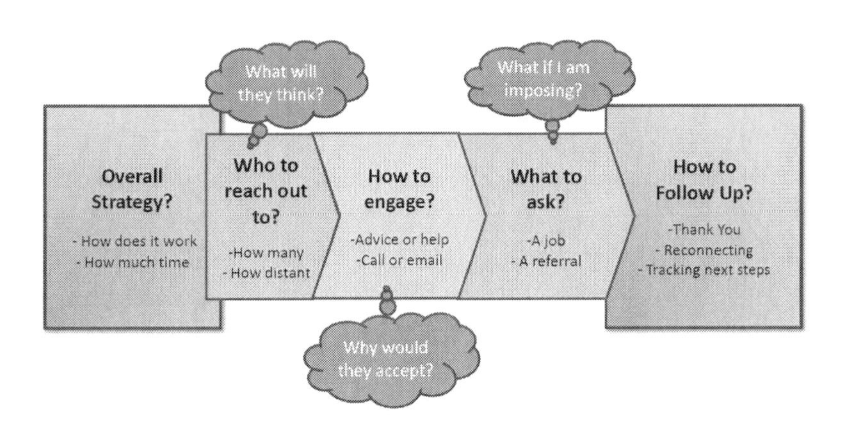

The fears that cause Networking Paralysis are almost all unsubstantiated. They tend to fall into every category of who, what, when, why, and how. I will discuss the answers to these questions in more depth in the third section of this book. For now, I will provide only the short answers:

- Who: Influential people you have a connection with
- What: You are asking for an in-person meeting—coffee is best, somewhere public, rather than in that person's office
- When: As soon as it is feasible
- Why: They will meet with you because they want to help; you are asking for their help because you need connections
- How: A brief phone call or an email are the best way to request the meeting
- Topic: You are asking for career advice. Even though your goal is to get a referral, you should not say that up front

Now, we should focus on being proactive. Armed with the understanding of these logical points discussed above, many people still have trouble asking for meetings, even though they know a number of highly influential people in their world of direct or indirect personal connections. The last hurdle to overcome is the sense of vulnerability people feel when asking for a favor–it feels weak to open up about looking for a new job. This is an example where intuition steers most of us completely wrong, because when somebody does something that has some vulnerability, people perceive that as strength and confidence!

Sharing a vulnerability = showing personal strength

This inexplicable gap is something out of which Tony Robbins has made a lifetime business. Tony Robbins has been the most prolific personal success self-help expert for the last fifteen years. He explains that the inability to actively seek help is a result of "negative neuro-associations,"[3] whereby we subconsciously create the association of something negative to a particular activity. The negativity tends to revolve around a fear, perhaps in the subconscious, where your emotional self says "no," but your logical self says "yes." It is the gut-check that steers you the wrong way. It is the inner compass that may be off target, pointing in the wrong direction.

Tony Robbins has dozens of techniques to help people through this conflict of logical versus emotional/subconscious self. From my understanding of his principle, the essence is to focus on decision-making. It may help you to answer the following questions: What decisions are you making right now that can change your life forever? What decisions are you making every day that create opportunities? What decisions are you making that enable you to reach your goals? Tony's insight is that these negative neuro-associations steer people in the wrong way in all the key elements of their lives—professional choices, personal relationships, etc.

Not everyone needs to attend courses Tony Robbins holds, as some people are so bullish on their goals and so confident that they intuitively make assertive decisions on a regular basis. But even the most confident people could benefit from the self-reflection on

3 *Awaken the Giant Within,* by Anthony Robbins

how they are making decisions. Referring back to your inability to seek help, if you assess the situation logically, you will realize that there is nothing to fear. There is no logical reason for you to *not* take the step and ask for a meeting.

Success requires action. It begins with the understanding that it is not only okay to ask for help, but it is a win-win for you and the people you approach. And it's about living the philosophy.

Key Takeaways:

- Nobody is successful alone
- Successful people want to help, and they are flattered when you ask
- Involve others willingly in your job search knowing they will see you as a strong and confident person taking charge of your career.
- Don't let negative neuro-associations stop you from connecting with the people who want to help

CHAPTER 3

The Uncertain Job Seeker

While some know exactly what they want to do for their ideal job, many people don't. If the only clarity you feel is that you don't want to do what you were doing in the past, then you have some decisions to make! The good news is that most people go through this kind of uncertainty in their career at one point or another.

Chapter twenty focuses on the key steps to take when you know the direction you want to take if you are changing professions and you need a plan that will help you get the job you want. This chapter helps those still facing indecision reach a decision about the next target job.

What is your passion?

The problem with the "passion question" is that people who are naturally inclined to find things that they are passionate about don't need to be reminded of this. And the people for whom passion does not come so effortlessly get tired of hearing the mantra of "find your passion."

I'll share what work-related passion means to me. It means that you see your work as your personal mission—a mission where you are on a path of focus and energy that you can't get out of your head. When you are passionate about your work, you wake up thinking about ways to solve the complex problems that remained when you left the office the day before. Working in a job that fulfills you means that you are excited when you have a new idea that can help the company, and you can't wait to tell the others on your team. It means that when you make the step-by-step progress towards big milestones, you feel a deep sense of gratification and impending future greatness. It means that the problem you are working towards and solving becomes a reflection of yourself and you show it off with pride. You see the accomplishment as proof that you are on a worthy path and it validates the continued pursuit of your mission. Working passionately means that you see, with great clarity, what achieving the goal looks and feels like. It is the relentless pursuit of achieving that goal, and the continued validation in your own mind of the worthiness of that goal, that fuels the tenacity required to fight through any obstacle along the way.

Sounds familiar? If so, you are lucky to have had that experience in the past. Moreover, you know deep down that you need to get to that place again.

None of the above sounds familiar? Then you may have a number of different reactions to that paragraph.

One reaction to my interpretation of work passion could be that, even if you have heard of people that managed to get to that place, you still have a hard time imagining yourself being there.

Another reaction could be that you have been on the cusp of that sense, but have not found that thing that has pulled you all the way there.

Here's how I think about it. If you have been in that place of focused passion and personal purpose that drives you relentlessly to accomplish certain goals, then your job objective must be to get there again. It's a level of intensity of personal involvement between your ego and your ideas where any lesser level of intensity will leave you feeling less than fulfilled.

If you have not felt that (and it is about feeling and not about thinking) then you may want to think about the relationship between work and passion from a completely different perspective. Rather than trying to find a personal passion, think about it from a team perspective instead. Your most rewarding career could be in a job where you get to do something that leverages your best talents with a group of people that you really like working with. When people find a supervisor and a team that share an excellent chemistry, great things happen. And it's fun. Not everybody can see themselves on a mission to save the world, but everybody likes being productive and working as a part of a great team.

The qualities noted above often equate to that combination of factors that cause people to define their job as "great." The right supervisor will recognize your strengths and make sure that you are assigned the right kind of work and responsibilities that utilize those strengths to their full potential. The right team will naturally be positive, funny, and encouraging. You'll have to do real work, but if you are doing something you are good at, you get the satisfaction of accomplishing and growing, and doing it in a fabulous environment.

Almost everybody I talk to says that their favorite work experiences have been when they worked with a team of fun, smart, energetic and just plain good people. It's hard to go wrong when you choose the people well.

So if this is you, consider your job search to be about finding that optimal work environment where you also utilize your favorite skills and talents. It's not as much about finding an exact position, title, or industry, as the focus in on the team and the company.

Some things to look for:

- A growing company: Companies that are growing tend to create positive energy and work environments more naturally. Companies that are struggling often have a hard time keeping a positive work environment because there is so much pressure to address the business issues, and they frequently have a looming fear of layoffs.
- A great supervisor: Ask your personal connections about who their favorite supervisor is/was, and then try to meet that person.
- Happy employees: As you meet with personal connections, inquire about the employee turnover rates at their company and others, as this is a good indicator of job satisfaction.
- Medium to small companies: A leader in a medium to small company that is growing typically sets a great tone of teamwork and respect that permeates the company culture.
- Large corporations can have amazing chemistry and momentum, and the right team within a large corporation might be right for you. The bonus of big company experience is that it looks good on a résumé, as big companies have clear reputations, mostly good, for hiring quality people.

Avocations rarely make good professions.

After experiencing the kind of job that leaves you with the conviction to change career direction, people are frequently on the "job rebound." Job rebound is that mental stage when you picture your dream job as some blend of your favorite hobbies and dream adventures. There is even a website now that points people towards the intersection of fantasy and work, which may be right for some people.

The typical outcome for people jumping off to do their fantasy job is that they find that the fantasy gets old very fast. I worked at Wilson Sporting Goods, first as the CMO and then as head of the golf club group. At first, I felt that this was the definition of a fantasy job, as we made products for every sport and sponsored dozens of top sports celebrities. What I learned was that the people who had the most fun with the sporting goods industry were the doctors who took Wednesdays off to play golf. The business of sports did have some perks, but it was a rough business marked by offshore discount manufacturing and dominant retailers that choked us at every turn. I didn't feel that I was building anything of any great meaning, as I spent most of my time fighting a share-of-market and profit margin war that was as tough as or tougher than any other business I have been involved with.

The point is this–job rebound is natural, and yet it often points people to an extreme that seems too good to be true, and often is. The real challenge is to decide whether you are going to commit to the pursuit of your passion, or, if you can find that blend of team and company growth that creates the optimum supportive work environment.

Nothing is permanent

Avoid decision paralysis by reminding yourself that nothing is permanent. On occasion, we get a job offer that feels so right that we don't even need to think about it. However, in most cases, not all our requirements will be met and we have to decide where to compromise. If some of your most important factors are in place, but not all, then it's often worth the risk to dive in. You will be surprised how many different types of work can end up becoming something you would come to describe as an ideal job.

People have the key

The power of the human mind to see possibilities and to make conceptual matches between your unique skills and desires and the 50 or 100 jobs that they know of and can perform well is the force that can get you to your goal. Rarely does time on the computer result in clarity or big ideas that point you in a new direction. The many dimensions of work and jobs are far too complex in their subjectivity for an internet site to capture, yet people solve these challenges naturally. In fact, they just can't help it.

Just to put your task into a perspective, remember that there are something like 5,000 different kinds of jobs, and that most of us only have an appreciation of no more than 50 of them. But when you add the variable of the culture of individual companies and the personality styles of different leaders, the number of different types of experiences you can find is almost infinite. Luckily, your connections can articulate with great depth their perspectives about the companies they have worked in, particularly in regard to the qualities of team and culture of positive energy.

Action Step Implications

If you are going to pursue the great company and great team angle, then you have a few choices. Choice #1, you can frame your current skills as the most likely job that you can be hired for, and begin a full job search. Just keep in mind that you are on a mission to find that excellent company and excellent team. Choice #2, if you are not sure what skills or job definition to pursue, then focus your energy on putting more definition around your target job. In this case, carefully read Section III of this book, chapters 10 through 16, as they are all applicable to your process of self discovery. These sections will provide a framework for connecting with people and framing your strengths, and by following these steps, you will are likely to arrive at a better understanding of what you want to do, and/or find that excellent team and company that will be the right next-best move for you.

Key Takeaways

- If you have a passion and you are not pursuing it, your time to change is now.

- If you don't have a driving passion, don't sweat it, most people don't. Instead, find an amazing team and an amazing company and dive into the job that best fits your skills.
- In both cases, your mission is to uncover a job to pursue. The best way to do that is to meet with your personal connections as well as influential and connected people. Somebody in your network most likely already knows about a job you would be thrilled to get.
- Nothing is permanent! Avoid decision paralysis and determine the most important qualities that you want to see in a company, then don't be afraid to dive in.
- If you are not comfortable beginning a job search for a specific role, focus on section III in this book to work through exploratory meetings to let people help guide you.

CHAPTER 4

Understanding How Hiring Actually Works

The most important part of a job search strategy is the ability to see it from the viewpoint of the hiring manager. Job seekers rarely do this, as they tend to focus on a company and a position, trying to fit their qualities, skills and experience to the job requirements. In doing so, they fail to appreciate that the hiring manager is the one that makes the decision, and hiring managers follow a predictable pattern.

But before looking into the mind of the hiring manager, consider that the person hired usually does not match the job spec very closely. This can be rough for the candidate who was told that he/she possessed the skills that fit the job well, yet failed to get the offer. At face value, this may seem odd. With all the digital technology parsing and classifying résumés, and HR departments delivering the best matches, where do things go off track?

If we look at the real decision-making criteria that hiring managers apply, we need to consider two dimensions: the opportunity of finding a great person versus the risk that the new hire will not perform. All hiring managers make this assessment, even if they have not defined the criteria with this specificity. It's primarily about trust—trust that the person coming in will bring the skills, rather than causing problems.

Remember, new hires can be a problem for many reasons. Most obviously, they may not have the skills the job requires. They may have the functional aptitude but not the people skills. Plenty of people in the world have great expertise, but if others find it hard to work with them it's hard to find a fit for them in a company. Some people have ethical or moral challenges that make their role as an employee difficult. I refer to these as "challenges" rather than "problems," because many people don't have a clear compass and decide for themselves whether their attitudes are acceptable or not. There are many individuals whose personal problems make a productive work life hard, such as substance abuse, family troubles, or psychological challenges.

Real or not, the perception is that unemployed people may be out of work for a reason, and the risk is that you hire such individuals for the upside reasons, missing the potential downsides. To make matters worse, both the law and human generosity tend to hide these problems and send people on their way. There is no way to conduct a background check for many of these issues. Individuals cited as references will most likely not know about them. Back-channel checks may not reveal these issues either. Employment problems are greatly held secrets, and hiring managers are mostly aware of this issue. Why? Because ALL hiring managers have experienced the excitement of betting on a great person that they "found" only to discover that the person was a problem and had to be let go.

With this new perspective, can you begin to feel the weight of the challenge the hiring manager is facing when selecting a new employee? How does he or she get through this? At the end of the day, they trust their gut—their sense of confidence that the person who is offered the job represents big opportunity with reasons to believe they are not going to be a problem.

So what does this mean for you? To understand more about how to plan around this, you should first appreciate that there are four different kinds of candidates a hiring manager sees: people they know, people who come from a highly trusted referral, people who come from a general referral, and people who are found. Think of it as a "trust scale," where the people who are known have the highest amount of trust, and the people who are found have the least.

Candidates in the Eyes of the Hiring Manager

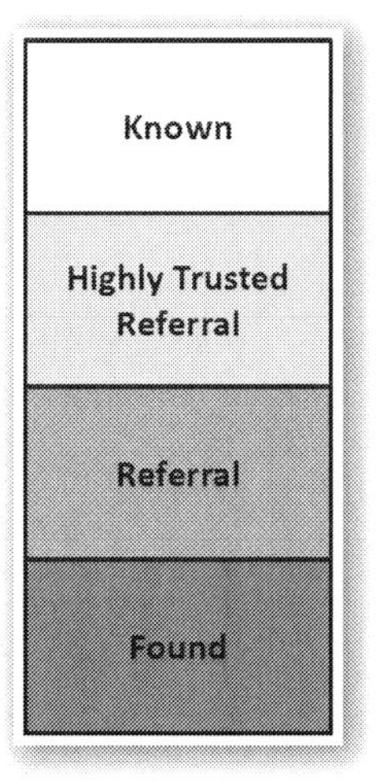

Known Candidates

The known candidate is the least risky for all the obvious reasons. When a hiring manager knows someone that he/she also thinks is a great skill fit for the role, very often the job is filled immediately without a selection or review process. But when the known person is considered to be good but not great for the role, he/she is often kept in the running while a search is started for a candidate who would provide a better fit for the job.

Highly Trusted Referrals

These candidates are proposed by people the hiring manager knows well—such as an expert in the same field, or the prospective candidate's former colleague or employer—and hence, the person comes with a "pre-qualification" of excellent skills.

The fact that there is a referral at all suggests a character reference regarding the lack of other problems that could represent a risk. Depending on the strength of the hiring manager's relationship to this person, and the hiring manager's perception of the referrer's skills, this referral can be as strong as the "known" candidate.

General Referral

These candidates are typically identified by people that the hiring manager knows but perhaps not very well. Alternatively, it is from someone that the hiring manager knows well, but it is more of a character reference than an endorsement of skills, based on the differing skill set of the referrer. These people are seen as more risky than the candidates from the two categories above.

Found

These candidates are found through some combination of résumé search and job applications submitted. They often have a very strong alignment of skills to the job spec, as that is the primary reason for identifying them among thousands of options. They are most often screened by HR personnel and included in the group of five or ten other well-screened candidates. The challenge is that these candidates could be frequently looking for jobs or currently out of work, and as such, with no internal referrals, they fall into the highest risk category. The candidates selected in this manner are frequently overqualified for the jobs, but are interested because they urgently need work.

The chart below depicts the way in which candidate introductions to a company affect the hiring manager's level of trust and confidence. This shows how personal connections, recruiting firms, and career sites/job boards relate to the trust scale.

Candidate Source and Hiring Manager Trust

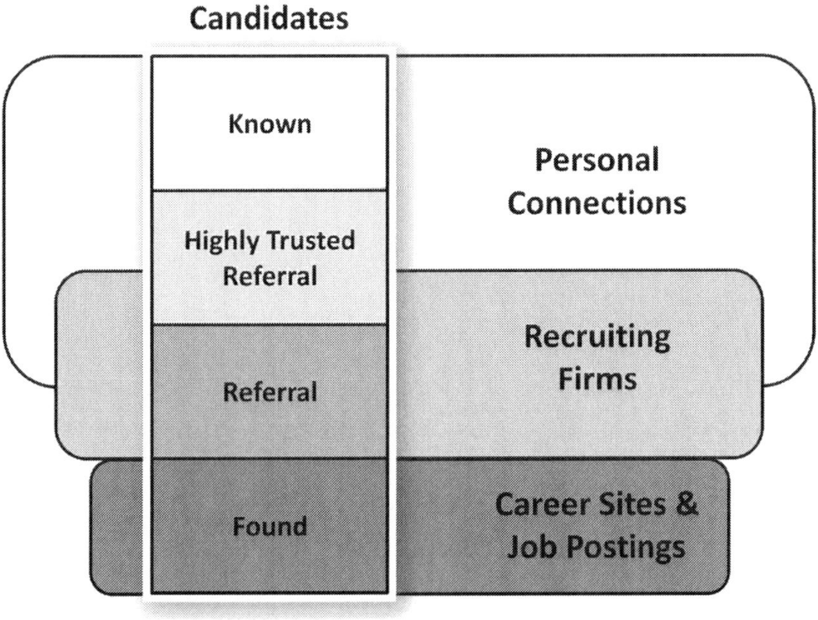

Candidates

Known

Highly Trusted Referral

Referral

Found

Personal Connections

Recruiting Firms

Career Sites & Job Postings

With this as background, the hiring process and results come into focus. The hiring process starts with a detailed specification of all the skills the applicant for the role should ideally possess. The HR department determines the skill set and uses it as the criteria when selecting a group of candidate résumés that provide the closest fit. At the same time, internal employees and other "known" candidates are in consideration, as well as individuals suggested by highly trusted referrals.

Through the process, the best candidates are asked to an interview(s), after which the decision is typically made between two or three candidates. But which two or three are the best choice? Whether it is conscious or not, it often comes down to the known or highly referred candidate who is not exactly the ideal skill match, and another candidate with a better skill match. Rather than having a magical person who is the most trusted and the most skilled, a hiring manager ends up with a conflict. Do we chose the person who inspires the highest confidence overall (i.e., we are confident that they will not be a problem employee), or do we take a risk on a person whose résumé indicates excellent skills?

Most often, the candidate who is known or who comes from the highly trusted referral gets the job. The risk of a problem represents a bigger downside, and the opportunity for a great person is an important upside. In other words, the risk of a problem is a more important decision factor than the opportunity of a great skill fit.

Easier to Get the Interview, and an Easier Interview

It is easier to get an interview if you focus your search in the top two boxes and not the bottom box depicted in the chart above. If that's not enough to convince you, consider that you will also have a MUCH easier interview if you know the hiring manager or if you come from a highly trusted referral.

Interviewing a known candidate tends to be more of a frank conversation than a formal assessment. None of the aspects of a typical interview apply. There is no need to try to get a feel for a person's communication style and intelligence, or your chemistry with that person. This kind of interview is just not hard.

In the same vein, interviewing a candidate who has come from a highly trusted referral feels more like a mutual introduction of a new friend than a tough interview. The interviewee still needs to sell him/herself, but will be greeted with a pleasant attitude, fewer tough questions, or maybe no questions at all. If the referral is quite strong, the prospective employee may be seen as someone who the hiring manager needs to convince to join, in which case he or she may talk most of the time. This is not hard.

Easier to get the interview. Easier interview.

Be Considered for Bigger Jobs

Very often people leave jobs because they feel stifled. They don't feel that they are being given the responsibility that they are ready for, and they become bored in a position. This is the natural order of life, and unfortunately, companies just don't have enough positions or openness for frequent movement to optimize everyone's careers. So as you work, you grow, and as you grow, you expand your potential and the clarity of what you like to do and what you would like to do next. This is part of the regular journey of seeking your ideal job.

Now, imagine that you are the hiring manager. You are interviewing a candidate who is an analyst seeking a more senior position, such as a manager. If you know that candidate, there's a comfort level and little downside risk with regards to personal problems and professionalism. Your only consideration is whether this candidate has the natural talents a managerial role requires. Very often, the hiring manager will know—based on the maturity and depth of the interviewer's answers—if he or she is ready for the next step. The point is that the focus is on whether you are ready for more, rather than whether you are a risk to the company.

Next, you have a candidate who was referred to you by a highly trusted friend with a high degree of relevant expertise. The referral comes with a strong endorsement that says something like, "This candidate is very strong, ready for significant level of responsibility, and if I had an opening I would hire him/her myself." The simple fact of referral is a personal character endorsement (deserved or not) that the candidate is not going to be a risk to the company. But more importantly, the endorsement gives you enormous confidence that the candidate can do the job. In other words, you are facing low risk, yet big opportunity.

Now, imagine a candidate who wants a bigger job title and a more challenging role than they have had before, but this candidate was "found" through a résumé submission/application. You are straining to get a feel for the candidate's readiness for a bigger job. You may be working hard to decide if the person in front of you can even do the lower level work well. Then you are trying to get a feel of the stability, reliability, and professionalism of the person, while assessing the risk they could represent.

Working against the candidate is something called the Peter Principle, which reflects that companies frequently promote people to the level to which they are incompetent. These people almost always end up leaving and looking for something bigger. The hiring manager has to wonder if the candidate is not only qualified for the job he or she is applying for, but if the candidate is qualified for the level below that. Because of all these risks, it is very hard for a hiring manager to put a "found" person into a big job. For these same reasons, it is also very common for people who are found to only be offered positions below their prior roles.

My story

As I reflect back on my various interviews and jobs over the years, the essence of the "found" versus "known" principle rings true. Every job I got that I felt was a good move up and was with a great company came from a trusted referral. In between these positions, there were a few jobs that were less than stellar, with less exceptional companies, and I obtained them without a good qualified referral. If only I had known then what I know now! The interviews at the best companies were of a different flavor—I could feel that I had a bit more respect. I had a feeling that they had been told something along the lines of, "Scott has options, and we'd be lucky to get him."

This was diametrically opposed to the feeling you have when you show up at a less-than stellar-company, and you see in the eyes of the interviewer a sequence of thoughts: 1) If this guy is so great, why is he interviewing with us? 2) If this résumé is true, and this person is here in front of me, what is wrong with this guy?

The answers were often as simple as "the recruiter convinced me to come over," nothing more and nothing less. I was also fortunate that a wise executive recruiter shared with me a very simple concept: "You have no idea if you would be interested in a company until you have met the people, discussed the job, and understood their growth strategy." With this in mind, I would look with curiosity at atypical companies for my career track. The important thing to note is that these were often brutal interviews, with worse companies and worse jobs.

I don't know of anyone who hopes to get a tough interview at a mediocre company for a job that is beneath them. Hence, you will see the main theme of this book is to understand how to easily generate trusted introductions to the companies and jobs that you can be excited about.

The Importance of Company Fit

In the process of interviewing, both sides are trying to determine if there is a good fit. I see "fit" as being a combination of:

- Functional expertise
- Industry expertise
- Passion for the company and the role

If you bring knowledge to a company from the industry or functional arena, then you are a skill fit. But the passion and, within that, the assumption of cultural and personality fit, is the softer aspect of the fit. One of the issues you will need to consider before attending your interview is whether there is an overt "passion profile" the company is looking for. When I was coming from the sporting goods industry for an interview at Microsoft, everybody kept asking me if I "loved" software. At first, I thought these people were a bit off their rocker, but I realized that this was the cultural rallying cry to help people align passion with their work. Boy, did I love software!

I now refer to this as a company's "passion profile"—that common thread of personal, emotional connection to the company and the industry. This is not a trivial matter, such as when a company has a culture shaped around shared "emotional" beliefs. You'll need to decide for yourself if you can sell others on your alignment, and believe it enough to feel that you are in the right place. It is commonly reflected in a sincere, personal interest in what makes that industry tick, where the opportunities are, and ideas on how you can be a part of championing a big change.

Understanding a company culture is not trivial, because strong companies take on cultures that typically have two elements: 1) a belief that their company is the best in the world, and 2) a common bond in the personal excitement and passion to tackle the toughest problems in that industry. Your hiring managers will have these cultural elements as core internal beliefs, and you need to make sure that they know that you, too, are in that mindset. If and when the hiring manager feels that you are a good cultural fit with the company, it is much easier for them to see you in the job.

Key Takeaways:

- Hiring managers define job requirements as a set of specific skills, but they hire based on trust
- Personal connections establish a basis of trust
- Interviews will be easier to get, and easier to do, with personal connections
- You have a better shot at a much better position with a personal connection
- Seek to understand your hiring manager's culture mindset—passion profile—and adapt

CHAPTER 5

Résumé and Interview Preparation

Writing your résumé and interview preparation is not very exciting. Because of that, although both are critically important, they get less attention from job seekers than they should.

The Résumé

Your résumé *must* have a professional, well-formatted look, and it *must* be error-free. People who have mistakes in their résumé rarely get interviews, as they imply lack of competence and attention to detail. Here are the most important elements I look for in a résumé:

1. Clean, crisp, and professional formatting.
2. Simple, clear, and direct writing. Avoid flowery adjectives.
3. Clear organization. I prefer the reverse chronological style, but a skills-based style can also be effective.
4. One page is sufficient for people with less than ten years of work experience, two pages should be used by people with less than twenty years' experience, and three pages are suitable only for senior executives with extensive and versatile experience.
5. Descriptions of job positions should be equally split between the position responsibility and the accomplishments, which should be quantified wherever possible.

What are hiring managers and HR departments on guard for in résumés? Lies. Different studies indicate different levels of "mistruths" in résumés, but many show that twenty-five percent of all résumés a company receives include one or more substantial lies. People lie in résumés to make them look better, assuming that, without the lie, they won't be considered, and hoping that they won't be caught.

This didn't work out very well for Scott Thompson, the once CEO of Yahoo! whose résumé included a computer science degree, which he did not possess. When the lie was discovered, he eventually lost his job. The members of the Yahoo! board of directors who hired him were embarrassed, and it was a black mark for the premier executive search firm Heidrick & Struggles that presented Thompson as a candidate to the Yahoo! board.

As a side-note, Thompson made an excruciatingly bad error in judgment when the lie was discovered and the media covered the snafu, as he blamed Heidrick & Struggles for changing his résumé and adding the computer science degree. This was not seen as plausible, and prompted Heidrick & Struggles to counter his claim with a stern denial. This was perhaps the most known example of repercussions for lying on a résumé in recent years, and a reason for caution HR departments should exercise. If a person with that level of visibility and scrutiny can get hired with mistruths on his résumé, just about anybody can.

There are many degrees and dimensions of lying. Some studies use a more stringent evaluation, which includes gross exaggerations and counts those differently than lies. For example, someone might say that they rolled out a new product that contributed to the company's growth of over seventeen percent in the subsequent years. Yet, when the details are pulled out, that product may not have sold well at all, falling behind the sales of the product it replaced, and hence, repressing the company's growth rate, not enhancing it. These gross exaggerations are found in as many as fifty percent of résumés. Half of all people will give themselves an enormous amount of credit for things that they may have only distantly touched. HR departments and hiring mangers know this, and when the results on a résumé sound too good to be true, that person is seen as being out of touch with reality.

In order to ensure that you are in the best possible position, you should follow the steps outlined below.

First, if you can afford it, retain a professional résumé writing firm. The additional polish and balance of strong statements that do not seem overstated is often the difference in the perception of the quality of the person. This is very important, because:

A quality résumé indicates quality person
A poor résumé says poor performer

If you cannot afford a résumé writing service, follow one of the many good résumé formatting examples available online. Some examples are provided for you below, as well as in the appendix of this book.

Second, have your résumé reviewed by three or four people who are close to you and are also working in the business, as they will be both interested in providing advice and suggestions for improvements as well as competent to do so. Listen carefully and thank everyone for their opinions. As you will likely get many different suggestions, you should apply only those that you feel would result in strong improvements. If you are using a résumé writing service, you should discuss this feedback with them, as they will be able to help you determine which elements to include.

Third, something that can help you in the interviewing process is to have your résumé "verified" by a company that specializes in résumé verification. Résumé verification companies check your academic background, your prior company employment dates, and other facts. They are in the business of being reliable, so most

HR departments will consider having a verified résumé a bonus. This is less important when you focus on obtaining a job through personal connections, but is a terrific added benefit that helps the company see you as solid.

(SAMPLE REVERSE CHRONOLOGICAL RESUME) *This is the standard option for most people. It is best for people with jobs that are in different categories and with different/increasing levels of responsibility.*

Jane Doe
Jane.Doe@dmail.com

238 Ashbury Street
Richmond, VA 23223
804-300-5000

<u>SUMMARY</u>

In this section list a high level summary about who you are. Include a top level description of your overall level, your areas of specialization, your best strengths, and a message about how you deliver results. This section is typically two or three lines for new grads, or 5-6 lines for more senior execs. e.g. Senior Marketing Research executive with extensive experience in leading large teams in both industrial and consumer products. Part of senior leadership team contributing to the creation of company strategic plans, identification of new business opportunities, and streamlining processes. Significant results in quantifying areas of opportunity in customer relations, product improvement, technical support, as well as numerous one-off studies. Specific strengths include detail orientation, analytic skills, complex study design and execution, and perspectives for long term strategic impact.

<u>EXPERIENCE (list in reverse chronology)</u>

Magnifico Inc. Houston, TX
Vice President, Marketing Research, (August 2009 to present)
• Describe the general business that the company is in. One line. e.g. Recruited to lead marketing research for this $11Billion company in the industrial valve category.
• Describe your areas of responsibility – two-three lines, be specific. E.g. Responsible for leading a team of 9 with a budget of $12.4M, in the creation and execution of marketing research across 6 product lines and 4 continents.
• Describe significant results, with data for each result. Two to four lines. e.g. Successfully contributed to the identification of three new product group categories, and helped form the customer value propositions for 4 new geographies. Completed 5 global surveys with key decision makers which has contributed to 6 customer service processes and manufacturing improvements in 4 plants.

Tribulator Co. Chicago, IL
Senior Direct. Marketing Research, (January 2006 to August 2009)
• Describe the general business that the company is in. This is meant to help the reader get some perspective about your work, there are thousands of companies and industries, so don't assume anybody knows your company
• Describe your areas of responsibility – If promoted to this position, list it. this is meant to help the reader understand what you have been entrusted with, and frame the scope of the results you should be able to achieve within your areas of responsibility. Beware of using acronyms, essentially, there should be zero three letter acronyms on your resume.
• Describe significant results, with data for each result. This is your chance to showcase your performance

Director, Marketing Research, (July 2004 to December 2005)
• Describe your areas of responsibility – When listing multiple positions within the same company, you do not need to list the description of the company's business, unless this role is a different division than the previous one listed.
• Describe significant results, with data for each result. This should be written in a way that shows such good results that it warrants the promotion or new role you had within the same company

Add all companies, or limit detail to past 20 years. If you have more than 20 years experience, just list the first companies and titles you had without taking too much room for accomplishments.

<u>EDUCATION</u>

MIT, Master of Science in Statistics Boston, May 1998
University of Norfolkshire, Bachelor of Science in Mathematics Becketts Bay, Maine, May 1995

(SAMPLE FUNCTIONAL RESUME-EXPERIENCED INDIVIDUAL) *This is a good option if the responsibilities, skills and results have been similar for many years of work in several different jobs. It is done typically to avoid having each company description sound like the one before it, none of which giving much depth. Consequently, the skill areas in this resume need to paint an excellent picture of capabilities and experience. Answer the question, what can this person do for me?*

JOHN Q. WORKER
14445 Ridge View
Laguna Beach, California 92812
(714) 555-1212
John.q.worker@ggmail.com

SUMMARY

In this section list a high level summary about who you are. Include a top level description of your overall level, your areas of specialization, your best strengths, and a message about how you deliver results. This section is typically two or three lines for new grads, or 5-6 lines for more senior execs.

SKILLS

Skill X: In this area describe a functional skill you possess. Give perspective about how many years you have been working with this skill, give dimension on how far along you are relative to the industry standards, share whether you teach this skill to others, whether you lead a team of others about this skill. List high level results with the skill.

Skill Y: Each skill should have a similar cadence to the description of the skill, the examples and the results

Skill Z:
5 or 6 major skills

EXPERIENCE
>> List in reverse chronology

Horatio Co. Wilkersonville, WY
Title, (August 2009 to present)
• Short description of the company, your responsibilities, and top level results. Unique info compared to the skills above and the other companies. No repetition! Should not be more than 2-3 lines of description per company.

Kolider Partners Healdsburg, CA
Title, (April 2007 to June 2009)
• Same

Include all companies since graduation – less and less description the older the companies get

EDUCATION

Bachelor of Liberal Studies in Business Administration May 2006
UNIVERSITY OF MARY WASHINGTON, Fredericksburg, Virginia

Continuous Improvement

You should ask the people you meet with to review your résumé and provide feedback throughout the process. Once your résumé has been scrutinized a few times, it should not have any glaring errors; however, you will get ideas about how to improve parts of it on an ongoing basis. Most people update their résumés every few weeks when actively looking for a job.

Customized Résumés

Depending on the organization and the job, you can consider customizing your résumé to fit the job description. I do not recommend spending too much time on résumé customization; however, as with the right personal connections, the precision of the résumé match plays less of an important role. The problem with customizing résumés is that you stand a greater chance of a typo or something that just does not look right. When hiring managers see errors in résumés, they tend to take the person out of consideration immediately.

Interviewing Skills

Some people are just naturally good at interviewing, while others struggle with it. Some people are natural connecters, observers, and very good at selling themselves, but not all job seekers are. Hence, you should view interviewing preparation as an opportunity to understand your own style and strengths in connecting with and persuading others.

A comprehensive guide on interview skills is beyond the scope of this book. Nonetheless, I have included an interviewing skills checklist in the appendix, and like to offer these tips:

1. First appearances and first impressions are as important as legend has it. You need to understand the professional level of the job you are seeking, identify the dress norms that company follows, and then dress one step above that. It is considered normal for the interviewee to be overdressed, and casual appearance is simply unthinkable.

2. You must be familiar with the product or service the company offers. The people you are going to meet live and breathe every detail of the product in great depth. Your familiarity with the product simply allows you to have a meaningful conversation during the interview. If you are not familiar with the company's main lines of revenue, you may get questions along the lines of, "Why are you here?"
3. Ideally, you will also gain some perspective about the industry and the competition that this company faces.
4. You must have a clear view of what your strengths are and be able to articulate them. You should also be very familiar with the requirements of the job you are applying for, and help the interviewer see how your skills are an excellent fit with the job description.
5. Be ready to discuss, explain, and expand upon every single item in your résumé. If you don't have a clear and compelling story that supports each part of your résumé, the interviewer will wonder if your résumé is completely truthful.
6. Listen. If the interviewer wants to talk through most of the interview, do not interrupt. People like to talk, so let them. Allow the interviewer to determine the cadence of the meeting.
7. Answer questions. Surprisingly, many people are so nervous in interviews that they start talking and fail to answer the question, and nothing frustrates an interviewer more.
8. Ask for the job! Hiring managers want to know that the person they are considering hiring truly wants the job. Practice saying things like, "I want this job," and "I can do this job, if you hire me, and you will be glad you did."
9. Practice basics of personal introductions and body language that conveys confidence. Make sure that your handshake is firm and look the person in the eye when you speak to them.

Before going on your first real interview, we recommend that you meet with some friendly business associates and ask them to conduct a mock interview. Most people, even those naturally good at persuading others, will have something that can be improved upon.

Some people will have a few major things to think about. Eye contact, confidence, clarity, brevity, posture, etc. all need practice. It is much better to get feedback before going into an important interview and address the issues raised than make mistakes when in truly matters. And, by the way, interviewers will not give you feedback on how to improve, even if you ask. Only the people you know will tell you the truth.

Key Takeaways:

- Your résumé must be mistake-free and professionally formatted
- Everything on the résumé must be verifiably true; companies are always on guard for lies
- You must be able to talk about and expand on everything in your résumé
- Interviewing requires planning and feedback from trusted associates
- Study the company and industry before an interview and be ready to ask thoughtful questions
- Ask for the job!

SECTION II

Get In The Game

There is a method that can be applied to kick off a job search in a powerful way—a way that gets you so much activity that you are thrown into the process of meeting, interviewing, and considering options in just a few days or weeks. In the following chapters, you will see how to tackle career sites and recruiting firms, and get your personal network connecting you to job opportunities.

CHAPTER 6

Career Sites

In this chapter, I will address career sites, also referred to as job boards. They include the largest Internet names in the jobs business, such as Monster.com, CareerBuilder, Dice, etc. I prefer to use the term "career sites" because they serve two primary functions. The first function is the organization and presentation of posted jobs—a true digital job board. The other, more important, function is a résumé board where people who want to be considered for jobs post their résumés.

Job Postings

If you are a college grad or looking for basic entry-level employment, go ahead and apply for posted jobs you would like to have. Better yet, identify the job that you would like to get and then see if you can find someone you know in the company to recommend you for that job.

For everyone else, ***the single worst way to spend your limited time is reviewing job postings and submitting applications and résumés.*** Here's why:

- First, as many as eighty percent of jobs come through personal connections[4]-many companies are prioritizing and

4 U.S. Bureau of Labor Statistics, various studies through 2011

structuring systematic ways to get referrals for candidates, both internal and external.

- Second, major companies hire scores of internal recruiters who are assigned to seek out and find the ideal candidates. These candidates are most often working at another target company.
- Third, external recruiters are hired regularly by most companies to fill the more senior roles, and these external recruiters focus on people who are currently employed.
- Fourth, many companies post jobs that they have already filled, just to comply with company posting requirements.
- Fifth, most jobs are not posted, so why compete with the thousands of people who are battling it out for every posted position?

Reading the above begs the question, if eighty percent or more of candidates are not hired through job postings, what is your chance of getting hired? Not great, unfortunately, because of the large presence of job boards, and the fact that people intuitively think that finding a job via a posting and applying for that job is a good use of time, millions of people do it.

When you consider the capabilities of technologies to help organize and automate the process of job posting identification and submission, you can see how the job applications spin out of control. Companies frequently receive 500, 1,500 or even 2,500 résumés per posted job.

Sometimes the intent of the posting is to follow a company policy to post jobs rather than a genuine need to find someone through the job board. When this is the case, there is often very little done to even attempt to review the résumés that come in.

When a job posting is placed with a real job search in mind, the target is to find just the right person that possesses the required blend of skills. As discussed in Chapter 4, the vision is that they would find a perfect person, with the combination of the skills and the "trust," or lack of risk, which a known person may represent. The challenge is to select a few résumés, among several hundred, for evaluation. This presents several challenges:

- First, it's almost impossible to review each résumé that comes through. As a result, yours is likely to be overlooked.
- Second, some companies use automated résumé analysis technologies to have a computer select the best-fit candidates. If you have used the right keywords, i.e. those that feature in the job description, you may be selected by the software. Many job search consultants advise people to match their résumé and cover letters to job postings so the computer will pick them.
- Third, there are often many "overqualified" people in the stack; as people who focus on answering job postings get more and more desperate, they start applying for any job.

If your résumé makes it through all these hurdles with the internal recruiting team, it is presented to the hiring manager along with five to ten others. The hiring manager will typically identify three or four prospective candidates for a phone-screening interview conducted by the internal recruiter. If you pass the phone screening, then you are brought in with the top few for a first round of interviews. Then if you pass that, you will likely be invited for a second round.

As I shared in Chapter 4, if you are invited for an interview, the hiring manager has identified you as the potential job candidate out of maybe 1,000 applications. That sounds promising, but it just means that you are the best of the ideal skill match group. The hiring manager will often have in mind someone that he or she knows, and still have some people who could be contenders who have been highly recommended.

Your task is not only to make them believe that you are a true expert in the skills they are looking for, but to make them extremely confident that you are a very low-risk hire. You wish to convey in the interview that you are reliable, committed, passionate, and fun to work with. These are the most challenging interviews to win. You need to give them as much evidence and ammunition to believe in you as you can. Offer to have them speak with former bosses. Ideally, these should be senior and credible people in business. If you can get them to call a few references that will be extremely persuasive about you as an employee, you have a better shot.

The best approach is to provide ample evidence about why you are a reliable and safe hire, but continue to feed the hiring manager's hopes—give ideas and suggestions for the kinds of work and accomplishments you expect to do in your first few months, so the hiring manager can strengthen his/her sense of opportunity. Ask for the job. Give an impassioned personal promise: "I promise to make you glad that you hired me, no matter how hard I need to work, no matter how hard the challenge."

Please, don't miss the main point here. Your chances of having your résumé selected among the pile is very small, perhaps one percent. If you pass this hurdle, your chance of getting to interview with the hiring manager is still small, perhaps twenty-five percent. Even then, your chance of getting the offer is also small, perhaps another twenty-five percent. Arithmetically, this is a tiny chance of closure—about one in 1,000. Worse yet, it is very unlikely that this job meets your skill level, and it's very unlikely that it is your ideal job.

Résumé Posting

The largest career sites also serve as résumé posting sites, and these include Monster, CareerBuilder, The Ladders, Dice, Indeed, and others. These sites serve as the largest database of "available" people in the marketplace, and tens of thousands of company recruiters search the top sites every week.

Uploading your information on the résumé posting sites is relatively easy, but updating your data regularly is a little harder. I suggest that people modify their résumé once every week during the period of active job search, taking advantage of feedback from people you connect with. With weekly or bi-weekly updates, it takes a fair amount of effort to ensure that you update your résumé in all the locations that you have it posted.

The top five positing sites get something in the range of ninety-five percent of all recruiter traffic, and I suggest that job seekers focus on those five, depending on the level of seniority and technical aptitude.

- Monster, Indeed, and CareerBuilder are most suited for people between entry level and director
- The Ladders originally targeted job seekers who are director level through VP level and recently expanded to include people with salaries at $40K.
- Dice is dedicated to technical jobs at all levels

Depending on your industry and profession, you may find that there is a niche job board that is regularly used by the recruiters in your area. The best way to identify such sites is to ask a few recruiters in your industry what they use, and if there are any industry-specific job sites that they find useful.

Beyond these leaders, there are another 500+ sites that are trying to break into the business, but since all the recruiters are reviewing the major sites, these sites make most of their money with ancillary services targeting the job seeker. There is a general rule of thumb in any given industry, where the #1 player in the industry extracts half of all the industry profit, the #2 player gets about a quarter, and the next three or four players get the rest.

The second tier sites are trying to earn their money in other ways. You may have experienced the negative effects of signing up for a job site, which begins a daily barrage of emails trying to sell you things like other job services, debt relief counseling, interview skills training, new books on getting a job, etc. Since posting on these sites is mostly free, they make money by selling access to their résumé database to recruiters, and trying to sell you something you most likely don't need. Consequently, résumé posting services that post your information on fifty to eighty job sites are helping these sites more than they are helping you.

My suggestion is that if a recruiter is looking for someone like you, in your town, with a company you like, you should be there for him or her to discover. This cannot be the only part of your search, as you may end up sitting by the phone for ages. Just post your data on the right career sites and move on with the more productive elements of your search.

LinkedIn

Everyone in business needs to be on LinkedIn, as it provides three important functions:

- A directory of business people—you can be found by many, and you can find most people
- A professional connection site—keep track of people you know, and have some visibility to the people they know
- A recruiting site—LinkedIn is now the preferred way to search for candidates, with thousands of recruiters viewing the site regularly

Within these three elements, there are a few things a job seeker should do:

- Send "link" requests to as many people as you know/can (for people you plan to meet with in the immediate two to three weeks it is best to send an email to ask for the meeting before sending the link request).
- Post your résumé.
- Use the contact list and the contacts' connections to beef-up your networking plan. Sometimes you need to see the people's names in front of you to remember or consider them.
- Frequently people you connect with know someone who could make a big difference in getting the right introduction. If you see a possible connection—meet with, or call (as in talk) the person you know and ask them about connecting to the person they know. Do not rely on the automated process that is built into LinkedIn—it's too impersonal, and few people respond positively to the all-digital connection requests.

If you are unemployed, don't go overboard with the services LinkedIn provides for job seekers. There is a fundamental problem—recruiters come to LinkedIn to find employed people. If they wanted to find unemployed people, it is far easier to go to the career sites. In time, we may find that LinkedIn takes over in this arena, as their current growth and standing in the industry suggests that this is possible in the near future.

Key Takeaways:

- ➢ Don't spend time applying for posted jobs, unless you are a recent graduate
- ➢ Your résumé and profile posted on the right career sites will make it easy for recruiters to find you
- ➢ Have a well-completed LinkedIn profile and résumé so that recruiters can find you

CHAPTER 7

Recruiting Firms

The recruiting industry is one of the most misunderstood parts of the job search ecosystem. I refer to it as the business of "Don't call us, we'll call you."Although thousands of recruiting firms are looking for great candidates for companies, they don't want you to call. To understand why that is the case, I'll first explain how they work, which is broken down into the three types of firms: Staffing Agencies, Contingency Firms, and Retained Firms.

Staffing Agencies: The staffing agency industry is mostly focused on temporary or part-time help at the lower levels of the company ladder, typically from administrative to middle managers. However, many staffing agencies are broadening their range into full-time and senior roles. Some people might not think of connecting with Adecco or Robert Half for their full-time job opportunity, but these firms have relationships with key companies and often get search assignments for key positions.

Staffing agencies are, by their nature, looking for local talent, in large numbers, so they have a good idea of whom they can quickly and easily present to a company.

Action Item: You should engage the staffing agencies in your area—you never know which ones are dealing with temp or full-time jobs that you might be interested in. Call or email to schedule an appointment. They will typically want to meet with you so they can get a feeling for your personal style and possible fit with one of their clients. The big firms like Adecco, Robert Half, Manpower, Volt, Spherion, and others may have something that works for you.

Contingency Recruiters: The contingency recruiting firms are defined as such because they only get paid when a person they have introduced to a company is hired. In other words, their fee is contingent on a hire. These firms often work in the upper middle management arena, but may also look for individuals suitable for executive roles. The challenge with contingency firms is that it is hard to establish what the relationship of the firm is to the client.

The more reputable firms have very strong relationships with their clients, and they have an agreement of exclusivity for a particular search. When this is the case, the contingency recruiter has influence over who is presented to the clients, and as such, has a higher probability of getting interviews for candidates that are contacted.

In the other end of the spectrum of contingency recruiting are the firms that try to throw as many people at a company as possible, as they don't have an exclusive arrangement, and it's a "race" among the various recruiters working on the assignment to see who can present the candidate that gets the offer. This is harder for candidates, as this résumé pitching is less discriminative and has a somewhat unsavory dynamic of "marking" a candidate (you) as theirs. In these cases, a contingency recruiter submits you to dozens of companies, and when you take a job at one of them, even if they didn't have much to do with your offer, they stake a claim on you for a placement fee. This can become uncomfortable for both the contingency firm and the candidate.

When talking with a contingency recruiter, it's wise to ask them what their arrangement is with the client. Even if it is a distant relationship, you may want to proceed, but just be aware that they might not know all the details about the job description or even the company and thus may offer you a role that is not suited for you.

Retained Recruiters: Most of the candidates for senior executive roles are placed through this type of recruiting firms, which include Heidrick & Struggles, Spencer Stuart, Russell Reynolds, Korn Ferry, and others. Retained recruiters charge a percentage of the first year's total compensation to conduct a search, and the fee is paid whether or not a person is hired. These firms have the best recruiters in the business, who have a unique ability to connect with employed senior executives and convince them to consider interviewing for a different company.

The top firms are chosen to identify candidates for the most senior positions of CEOs, CFOs, and board of director positions at top public companies. But the retained recruiting firms will also work on filling the most substantial VP roles, and sometimes for positions as low as senior director, depending on the company. At some of the largest corporations, titles can be deceptive, as a senior director at a Fortune 50 company is often a much bigger job than a VP at most other companies.

Action Item: Both contingency and retained recruiting firms simply don't have the time for engaging with you on your job search. Many people want to call their recruiting firm contacts, hoping to be selected for a role they may have been contracted to fill, but this is rarely effective. The statistics of the recruiter's task is too daunting to spend time on each candidate—of some 5,000 different types of jobs, industries, and levels, they need to identify the best five to ten people in the world for these jobs. Once they have narrowed down their selection, they target those people with calls and emails until they can get a conversation. They are looking for people who are practically one in a million.

Hopefully you now understand that, when you call a recruiter, he or she basically has to get you off the phone as fast as possible.

There is a zero chance that you are just the right person for their search. This is why I refer to recruiters as the industry of "Don't call us, we'll call you."

In order to make the recruiting world work for you, you will need to identify the best from the top 5,000 recruiting firms who handle jobs that are a fit for your level and your industry, and then get your résumé into their database. When recruiters do a search, they most often start with the people they find in their own databases. That's considered a quick win, and it's much easier than scouring LinkedIn or connections to find a match.

For you as a job seeker, contacting several thousand recruiters and submitting your data is an equally daunting prospect. Thus, you should rely on website support to make this easy, regardless of your level. BlueChipExec.com does exactly that, as it recommends the target recruiters (up to 500+) that conduct searches for jobs like yours and then it does the work to get you into their databases. Within a few minutes of your registration, you are "in play" and you can be comfortable knowing that you have done everything you can do to leverage the recruiting industry.

Key Takeaways:

- For executives and senior managers, match your background with the retained and contingency recruiting firms that specialize in jobs you are looking for, and make sure they have your résumé.
- For middle and junior level workers and individual contributors, staffing agencies will often have access to full-time and part-time roles that could be a fit. Get your résumés to them and see if their local office conducts interviews for prospective candidates.

CHAPTER 8

Personal Network Outreach

If you accept the fact that most jobs come through connections, and most companies place a high priority on internal referrals, then you will understand that the most effective thing you can do to kick-start your job search is inform your connections what you are looking for.

When you consider that most people are in close contact with thirty or fifty other people at any given time, then some of your contacts will certainly have heard of a job you might be interested in. If you reach out to 150 people, as many as five of them will probably have visibility to something that could work for you. Help them help you! If you connect with 400 people . . . even better.

I recommend sending a personalized email to your network with a link to your résumé. Attach your résumé only to notes sent to people you know well. For someone you are less familiar with, an attached résumé might feel awkward and appear a little desperate. Do not send an email with no way to connect to a résumé, as that leaves them little they can do about it. The letter should always be direct, friendly, and short; and don't forget to thank them in advance for their consideration.

Your Outreach Shows Strength, Not Weakness

It is in our nature to *fear* the idea of sending a note to our contacts informing them that we are open to consider new positions, and that we would appreciate an introduction. Many job seekers feel uncomfortable being so direct and their first reaction is to recoil at the idea. But why?

The main reason is that people are embarrassed to reveal that they are looking for a job. So first, keep in mind that you can't *both* get a job from a connection *and* not let your connections know you are interested in a new position. So embrace this fact that people who reach out to connections are seen as strong, confident people, who are taking control of their lives. Embrace this fact that when we share a vulnerability about ourselves, others see us as strong.

Sharing a vulnerability = showing personal strength

Imagine what the reader of your note is thinking–hmm, this friend is very proactive about taking control of his/her career...perhaps I should be taking control of my career as well. You could even write your introduction letter to that effect. Something like:

> Dear George,
>
> I've decided that I am only going to work in jobs where I feel excited to go to work, can immerse myself in leveraging my best talents, and can believe every day that I am working to create something of meaningful value. To that end, I am looking for a new role with a great company as an X, in the Y industry. If you or someone you know is aware of a job that fits that description, please let me know, or forward my résumé.

I was at dinner a few nights ago when a senior and influential friend told me about a note he got from another mutual friend, asking him for just such a connection. He said that he would get these "all the time," and was happy to help.

I want you to consider the fact that he gets these kinds of requests "all the time." I will share this point very simply, very clearly.

People who engage their networks get jobs fast and easily, and they have options.
People who do not engage their networks for fear of being thought of poorly
are frequently out of work for long periods of time.

Although nobody would have thought negatively about an employed person looking for a better job, being out of work for a long period of time gives others cause to wonder. Why so long? It is FAR WORSE to keep your job hunt to yourself and be unemployed than it is to engage the people you know and be employed.

Still not convinced?

Let's look one step further. Think of all the people you are going to send your note to as one of two types: contacts who like you, and the contacts that you think like you but don't.

Contacts who like you: The people you have in your contact lists who actually know you and do like you will see this as a confident and direct approach at taking control of your work life. Go ahead and tell them that you are on a personal mission to find your ideal job. Tell them that you are interested in matching the best of your talents with the company and the position that needs them the most. You will find that these people want to help you. People like to help others, and friends enjoy doing something that would benefit their friends. If they are working at a large company, they are asked all the time to make introductions and referrals. If they are working at a smaller company, they still may know of an open position, and they certainly know people that could be worth getting introduced to. It is simply the most natural of things to do.

Contacts who don't like you: Well, some of the people you are connected to due to similar job or other interests may not know you that well, or may even think negatively of you. Some may have competitive thoughts, but who cares? By *definition*, if someone is not open to helping and referring you, they are not your friend, so why bother having them in your contact list at all? If you are concerned that they will talk about you behind your back, imagine how they will feel when in six or eight weeks they receive the email from you announcing your new job! Isn't that a terrific trade-off? To be thought of badly by some of the "non-friends" in your contact list for a few weeks will make sending the "thank-you for helping me get this great new job" message even sweeter.

For more about this topic, I recommend people watch the 20-minute TED video (ted.com) featuring Brené Brown on the topic of Vulnerability. She also has a related video about shame. Like many ted.com videos, these are worth viewing regardless of your desire to find a job or not.

You Can't Know Who Your Contacts Know

When sifting through your list of connections, don't make the most common mistake of deselecting people based on their profession or your perception of whom they know. The fact is that *you can't know whom your contacts know*, as many dentists know many business people, and engineers know marketing executives, etc. We have even heard of one person's next-door neighbor who was in her eighties, but her grandson was a software developer, and hence, a great hire.

If you do deselect some people, make sure that you still send your résumé to the majority of people you know. However, do consider that every person you deselect may be the person who was going to connect you to a great job.

Key Takeaways:

- As many as eighty percent of new jobs are found through connections, so letting your connections know what job you are looking for is the quickest and most effective way to jumpstart your job search.
- People who find jobs quickly reach out to a broad number of their contacts the first day of their search. Those that do not reach out to their contacts at all are not likely to get a job.
- Include a link to your résumé, or attach your résumé in the email you send.

CHAPTER 9

Close Friend Endorsement Outreach

The next most effective thing you can do for your job search is to work with your five most trusted friends and have them reach out on your behalf to some of their most influential connections. It is a simple process where you meet with your friend, discuss some of the people in their network, after which they send an email to their connections that endorses you as a great candidate. The email should endorse you emphatically as a person of great character and skill in your field, and should always include a link to your résumé. This close friend outreach can be even more effective than the email you send to your network, as the endorsement from one friend to another carries the additional weight and importance.

Sample Letter: In this example, you are Harold Framington, and the friend helping you is Bob Walterson. This is a letter you, Harold, would share with your friend Bob to give him an example of the kind of note you would like him to send to his network:

> Dear [your friend's first name here]
>
> I hope that you are well. I am writing to you today to make you aware of a friend and exceptional person who is now in the job market. His name is Harold Framington, and he has an

outstanding background in global marketing and digital music rights management. I have known Harold for over 14 years and can attest with full confidence to his professionalism and ability to make great things happen. Any company would be lucky to get him. If you know of somebody who could benefit from his skills, please feel free to forward this note. Please find a link to Harold's résumé below.

[your friend's first name], don't hesitate to reach out to me or Harold directly with ideas.

Thank you for spending a few cycles thinking about this.

Sincerely, Bob Walterson

For an amazing boost and fast action for job leads, I strongly urge people to meet with three to five friends and have them send about twenty-five emails to the right people. Encourage them to select senior, influential, and connected people to introduce you to, providing you indirect access to 75-125 people who can make a difference to your career.

This close friend endorsement outreach can be quite effective. Here's why:

1. Within most people's business and social networks, they have perhaps twenty people they are very close to and can trust, and another fifty or seventy-five with whom they share mutual respect and occasional interactions. In total, there are probably 100 to 150 people that, when receiving an email of endorsement of another person, will take a minute to review the job seeker's qualifications, and apply a bit of effort to think of a possible action. Some may just file it away or forward it to their HR, while others may want to meet with you directly to discuss your options.

2. As with your own outreach, you just can't know whom your friends know, and as such, you shouldn't try too hard in advance to decide who is the right person to contact. It's about trusted relationships, not perfect, functional matches.

I have heard that some people are reticent to approach a friend in this manner, feeling that it is too much to ask. Well, at first blush it might sound like too much, but when you break it down, it's not:

Your Friends' Connections: One reason this is seen as being too much to ask is that it will be a burden for the people who receive the email, but that is completely wrong. *Perfectly* wrong, as I like to say. When somebody gets an email from a trusted friend about another trusted friend, that email is *treated with great respect and seen as an opportunity*. It is an opportunity for the receiver in many ways, based on the fundamental truth that finding great people is the hardest thing to do in business:

1. An opportunity to add a great person to his or her own team
2. An opportunity to help that person's company with a great new person
3. An opportunity to help another friend who may be looking for someone with these skills

In each case, there is only opportunity. If after careful consideration, the receiver cannot find a role for that person, rather than feeling that they have wasted their time, he or she may actually feel sad that they missed out on an opportunity.

Your Friends: When you explain the above to your friends, they will understand what you are trying to accomplish by asking them for help, as this benefits both you and their network. Besides, all you are asking of them is to email their twenty-five most trusted and influential connections.

Key Takeaways:

- An amazingly easy and highly effective way to accelerate your job search and put you in the running for great jobs is the close friend endorsement outreach
- It is truly a win-win-win—a chance for your friend to help you and his or her friends, an opportunity for the people that your friend reaches out to, as good people are always hard to find, and a win for you
- It is best to identify the twenty-five people together, and execute the mail at the same time

Conclusion

With this "get in the game" work completed, your work on the computer is done. You don't need to spend time with job boards, job postings, other career sites, or classifieds. You are set free. You are free to spend your time in a healthy, positive spiral of meeting in person with people who will amaze you, surprise you, enlighten you, and brighten your every day. These are people you know, but you don't have any idea how much they can do for you. You will, after reading the next section, titled "Get Connecting."

SECTION III

Get Connecting

The email outreach to your personal network is a good way to catch people when a job they have recently heard about is still on top of their minds, and generates timely, instant, and quick recommendations. What the email does not do is fully engage the people who have the most influence in helping you find a job. The introductions and advice that can be gained by reaching out to the most influential people is the most misunderstood and most underutilized of the job seeking steps.

In this section, I'll show you how to make the most out of connecting with people in your network in a way that is easy, energizing, and fun.

CHAPTER 10

The In-Person Meeting

I emphasize the importance of in-person meetings, because there is a critical dynamic to this type of interaction that is not present in a phone call or an email. This chapter explores all the reasons the in-person meeting matters, and it can be distilled down to the level of commitment you get from your contact to provide meaningful advice and connections. Nothing feels better than sitting across the table from someone who needs to find a new job and knowing you have the knowledge to help. The sense of urgency and the essence of generosity and giving are almost palpable. Few things matter more than work.

Who

You may be drawing a blank when you try to think of the charismatic, connected, senior, and influential people that you could reach out to, but when you think about it more, you might be surprised at how many individuals you identify. I suggest that you make a thorough list using this approach.

Personal

- Extended friend network
- More distant friends and acquaintances on Facebook

- Look through LinkedIn and see who your friends are connected with—you may find someone that you have met through that friend that you can reach out to
- Your best friends' professional networks
- Your parents' best friends that you have met
- Your parents' connections that you have not met
- Your aunts and uncles
- Your friends' parents, particularly if you know them well
- Neighbors
- Ex-neighbors
- Relatives of friends
- Friends of relatives
- Sports friends
- Church or Synagogue
- Classmates: high school, college

Professional

- Prior supervisors
- The supervisors of your supervisors that you knew, even if you interacted only occasionally
- Co-workers
- Clients
- Ex-clients
- Successful ex-subordinates

You get the picture. You need some kind of personal connection, and your world is broader than you may think. Consider why some people have as many as 1,000 or more LinkedIn connections–it reflects that people have a tremendous number of personal contacts.

To build your list, we designed a sample worksheet you can use to make it easier.

Identifying the Charismatic, Connected, Influential and Powerful People in Your Network

Close Friends Who Are Well Connected	Neighborhood Friends	Prior Neighborhood Friends	College and High School Friends	Influential Facebook and LinkedIn Connections
Parents, Friends and Connections of Close Friends	Aunts, Uncles, Cousins & Other Relatives	Prior supervisors, and supervisors of prior supervisors	Co-workers, Prior Coworkers, Clients, Prior-Clients	People Through Associations: sports teams, church, clubs

Why

The people who fit the description above will be willing to meet with you because they understand that everything happens through people. If they have a generally positive impression of you, they will agree to take the meeting. Even if they have a slightly "below average" experience with you, they will likely not turn you down, as an odd thing happens inside a person's mind when they are asked for a meeting. They will *re-define* you in their mind to be a stronger candidate, finding some strength or quality that justifies making the connection.

Remember, believe, and live the most important lesson:

Successful people want to help
They are flattered when you ask

This is important to understand and accept as the fundamental truth. The people who like you will bend over backward to help. The people who don't like you very much will still not turn you down. This is the zone of humanness that you should feel very comfortable to tap into. The vast majority of people have a soft spot when they are asked for help, so . . . ask!

If you are rejected by someone that you thought would meet with you, DON'T sweat it! It is typical for one out of five people to inexplicably deny you a meeting. Most of the time you won't know why, and the mistake people make is that they think they have done something wrong to hurt the relationship. Wrong again! You can't know what is going on in another person's life, and it's possible that the person may be having family or health trouble, job stability problems, or work issues. When people are in a state of personal crisis, they have a hard time carving out time to help others.

If you can, make sure that they got your message before giving up on them. Too often people send one email and assume they were rejected when in fact the person never got the email. I suggest that if you don't hear back from someone via email, send a brief follow-up a few days later, then call a few after that. Assume that they have not received your message until you know that they have. Besides, your tenacity may actually shake them free from their personal immersion, and you want to offer them the ability to feel good by helping another person.

What

Your goal with the meetings is to identify opportunities the person you are meeting with may have directly or through an introduction. Your secondary goal is to get advice on everything from your résumé to approaches and variations on your career that you may not have heard about. Remember that there are around 5,000 different kinds of jobs, and most people are only truly aware of 100 or so. Take time to listen about some of the other 4,900, many of which could be natural transitions for you from your current experience base.

The subjects you talk about are simple: you should focus on your skills, experience and expectations, and that senior person will share some stories and perspectives and will intuitively offer some excellent advice for you. Since you need connections, that senior person is likely to think of someone else you could talk to. The introduction from that senior person is an implied endorsement; it comes with a certain amount of risk on his or her part and a huge amount of responsibility on your part. We will discuss this important point later.

How

I stress the importance of the in-person meeting because there is nothing more effective for your career. I suggest that in-person meetings should be held in the morning at a coffee shop. You want to avoid meeting in the person's office because they have a much harder time giving you their undivided attention at work. Only agree to phone meetings if your contact insists on it, or if they are too far away. If it's a phone call, make sure that you schedule enough time—half an hour should suffice for a thorough exploration of your background and interests.

Your goal is to engage the person you are meeting with fully in your cause, in the vision of finding your ideal job. You want them to not only provide ideas and referrals at the time of the meeting, but you want them to feel good about coming up with more ideas for you over the next few months. Ideally, at the end of the meeting, you will start creating your own personal job search dream team.

Here's how it works: When you meet with someone in person, there is an implicit understanding that he or she is there to help you. The power of presence, eye contact, sharing a smile and a coffee is the beginning of deeper engagement. Since they are successful people, they don't quite yet know it, but they will soon be racking their brain to ensure they provide the best advice and connections that they can. If you fail, they will feel that they have failed, and successful people hate to fail, so they work hard to avoid it.

The ideas will come early and often, but they may not think of whom they can introduce you to immediately. That's because the more you share about yourself, the more they learn about what you are looking for, and the more information is going into their conscious and subconscious mind, generating fresh ideas. The conscious mind has most of what we think of as "top of mind" references. You may get some of these, but the subconscious mind is more powerful, because it is activated during a process akin to your conscious mind sending out thousands of tiny scouts to all corners of the brain to look for an answer. Since ninety-five percent of the decisions we make as humans is made by the subconscious mind, you want people to process your job search deeply enough to be absorbed by their subconscious.

Never forget your goal—you want to either get a direct lead, or one or two referrals. Referrals are either companies with direct hiring needs, or just well-connected people with more ideas for you.

Deeper Mechanics of the In-person Meeting

Your key task in the meeting is to follow a natural but purposeful flow to the conversation. Start out with normal pleasantries, connecting on a personal level. After ten minutes or so, you should break into the conversation about the search by taking charge of the conversation—"Thank you for agreeing to meet with me on this . . . here's what I am thinking." With a transition into your ideas, you need to describe with great clarity the kind of work you are looking for. "I have decided to focus my job search on a manager level position in product management with a medium-to-large-size technology firm." "I am most excited about these industries and this kind of environment, but I am also quite intrigued by this direction . . . ."

- Specificity in the definition of what you want in the first quarter of your meeting gives the person you are meeting with a clear idea of how they can help. They are thinking, "Okay, this person wants this kind of job, and now I know how to proceed."
- If you are not specific with the target job, the person you are meeting with is OFF THE HOOK and no longer responsible for a quality introduction, but instead, will freely offer advice and ideas for you. That's fine, if that is what you want, as it could be that you have not yet defined your search.

The person you are meeting with is now going through a brain scanning process that will occupy them until the end of your session together. It often works like this: First, they can't think of anything that can help you, so they often *qualify* their ability to add value by setting low expectations. "I'm not sure if I'll be able to do much for you, but let's see." This is a defensive move they have to make for the sake of their own ego. Their ego is suggesting that, if they set your expectations low enough, when they essentially fail to deliver good advice, you won't be too disappointed in them.

Interestingly, as this relieves the pressure they are feeling, it allows the subconscious to go to work on the problem, increasing the likelihood of success. I say subconscious, because that tends to be where their best ideas come from.

For the next two-thirds of your time together, the conversation will likely contain a discussion about the merits and options of the job you are looking for. This will typically lead to the combination of suggestions of what you can think about, what you can do, and a person or two that you could meet.

Somewhere in the last third of your meeting, very frequently a few "perfect people" for you to meet with "pop" into the person's head. This is the result of the subconscious tapping the mind and thinking through 400-600 possible acquaintances. It typically sounds like this: "Of course! I know exactly who you should talk to . . . ."

Make sure you that leave the meeting with a clear next step, and ideally the contact information of the person you are supposed to meet. After the meeting, it is a MUST that you send an email within twenty-four hours, thanking the person for meeting you. Snail mail is a nice personal touch, but it takes so long that people may feel unappreciated in the meantime. Writing a thank-you note means that this person will help you more, as you have noted your respect for his/her time and energy.

More Reasons to Believe You Need to Meet in Person

I can't emphasize the importance of the in-person meeting enough. The source of letting the enormous potential of the human connection work in your favor is in the meeting. People need these ingredients to be able to think deeply about how to help you, and these only happen in a personal meeting:

- The impact of personal presence, including eye contact and a smile
- Uninterrupted time to immerse themselves in your goals
- The "accidental" commitment to help you by virtue of taking the meeting

- Clarity about what you can do and what you want
- Feeling your personal sense of gratitude makes them want to do more for you

To optimize the outcome and allow their subconscious to work most effectively:

- Arrange morning meetings—people are fresher in the morning than in the afternoon, and you are looking for an alert mind
- Meet at a coffee shop—coffee is a stimulant that creates energy and optimism, and a coffee shop is an informal setting that not only takes them away from distractions, but also helps start the conversation on a topic unrelated to your job search
- Time—ideally you will have forty-five minutes or more, as if you are in a thirty-minute meeting; the first fifteen minutes is spent getting coffee and discussing pleasantries, leaving too little time for the immersion and human interaction that creates the subconscious brainstorm you want.

Inside the Mind of the Contact

From the perspective of the contact's desire to help, remember that they have tasked themselves to truly help you. That means that they are keen to offer something of specific value that can lead to a job. Hence, if they only provide advice and fail to make a quality introduction, they will feel bad that they have let you down.

This is important to understand when it comes to following up after the meeting. Here's what I mean: Many times you will conclude your meeting with someone, and they will promise to get back to you after they check with some people. These "let me look into it" conclusions are common and for the most part sincere. But these are also the kinds of things that slip through the cracks, so if you have not heard back from your contact within three-to-five business days, send them an email. Say something like, "Joe, I want to thank you again for spending time with me last week, and I would like to see if you have reached the person you mentioned in our meeting." This is perfectly okay! You are just prompting them to do what they promised they would do. No problem. They may even apologize for dropping the ball.

REMEMBER that they will not be happy until they have succeeded in their task to help you.

Meeting Frequency

The ideal search includes about ten meetings per week, which may sound like a lot, but is only two per business day. After four weeks, you will have had forty meetings that would result in something like thirty-to-sixty referrals. With all these meetings and all these introductions, the amount of ideas and leads can almost overwhelm you. That, by the way, is not a good thing; it's a great thing!

Key Takeaways:

- Since successful people want to help and are flattered when you ask, most will agree to meet
- In-person meetings engage your connections more deeply than they would through other means of communication
- In-person meetings build relationships, and relationships generate the trust needed for referrals
- You have far more people in your network to meet with than you know—it takes an exercise and worksheet to think of them all
- With two or three meetings per day, opportunities will appear faster than you can imagine

CHAPTER 11

Qualities That Get Referrals

For the majority of people, the information provided in this chapter is not news. However, I do believe even the most well-educated individuals can benefit from being reminded of the things you can do to make your contacts excited to refer you to others.

It's About Character

There are many small things that we do that we might not even be aware of, but do get noticed by others. The important thing about the small things—in this case I am referring to manners—is that it is a reflection not of your upbringing, but of your character. Manners were invented to create a standard of conduct that demonstrates respect and courtesy to the people with whom you come into contact. They are not just random rules, although some may seem that way.

Manners relate to character, because for the people who live by good manners, there is no way to tell if the person with poor manners is just ignorant or if they just can't be bothered to treat others with respect.

Yes, the impression can be that strong. You could present an excellent intellectual case for a referral, but your lack of manners could make such a bad impression that you will be left with nothing.

You might be thinking, well, I bet *my* contacts will be more understanding and overlook my transgressions. But if you've offended your contact, how can he/she in good conscience refer you to one of his/her friends? He or she would feel horrible thinking that you might treat his or her contact with disrespect.

First Impressions

Even if you know the person you are meeting fairly well, and even if you worked together in the past, when asked to meet you, he or she is going to see you through a different lens.

- Before the meeting day: Make sure that you have researched the companies and/or industries that you are targeting. A little knowledge and clarity will give your contact greater comfort that you are going to be a good fit for that industry, and he/she may have something meaningful to say to a referral.
- Preparing for the meeting: Based on your clothing and your grooming, your contact will have a feeling, an intuition, about the industry and role that would suit you. Like it or not, the world works on a dimension of "sameness" where new people need to dress, talk and walk like the people in the industry that they aspire to move to.
- Make sure that the place you have selected for your meeting has a clean and professional environment. Your favorite "dive" restaurant is not a good idea.
- You must be early, not "just on time." You have asked this person to take a part out of his or her day as a favor to you. If they arrive ten minutes early, and you are already there, you have made an even more productive use of their gift of time. If you arrive ten minutes late, and they arrived ten minutes early, you are not only guilty of being late, but the impression and the feeling that your contact is experiencing is one of wasted time and a touch of frustration. In other words, you just tipped their scale of "do I want to risk introducing this person to one of my contacts" toward "no."

- By being early, you have the time to decide on your order and, when your contact does arrive, offer to buy his or hers. You are the host, so you need to make every attempt to pay for the drink. A strange dynamic of our culture is that whoever buys has done a favor for the other person, for which the other person registers a small sense of reciprocal obligation. You want that dynamic in your favor!

The Conversation

- The "what" of the conversation is discussed in Chapter 10, but the first goal of the meeting is making sure you set a positive impression.
- Eye contact is essential. You need to convey your interest, your personality, and eye contact helps people relate in a generous way. Perhaps one of the biggest pitfalls of all the digital solutions is that there is no eye contact.
- Ask your contact about their family, job, and hobbies. This is a relationship-building process, which helps your contact connect with you on a personal level, and when they do so, their desire to help you will be generated.
- Make sure to listen—people like you more if you allow them to talk without interruptions.
- Keep the amount of food to a minimum. It's hard to have a deep conversation and a big meal and keep all the right manners in check. The issue of making sure that your mouth is closed while chewing, selecting correct glasses and flatware, etc., should not be on your mind when discussing your professional future. Few of us think that we have any challenges with table manners, and you may not, but minimizing the amount you eat helps bring that to a minimum.
- Don't be too presumptive with regards to introductions. Once you made it clear to the person you are meeting what you are looking for, if you mention someone that he or she knows that you would like to meet, and they do not

volunteer that person later, don't press the issue. You don't want to make the person feel uncomfortable.
- Offer to help this person with anything that seems logical.
- Thank the person with enthusiasm. When you conclude your meeting, you want to make sure that they "feel" how much you appreciate them for meeting with you and offering to make an introduction.

Follow Up

All the right follow-up elements are featured in Chapter 14 about building your job search dream team. Still, it is worth noting that the quality of your initial follow-up is immensely important. By demonstrating excellent communication and gratitude, your contacts will open their hearts and make more introductions for you. This is the essence of the dream team concept.

Remember that the people you engage during your job search process will become part of your job search dream team. But careers are a never-ending search for your ideal job, which is why this book focuses on the development of trust relationships that create opportunities that do not end at the conclusion of a job search and begin again with the next. It is important for you to stay in touch with everyone in your network who has helped you in a meaningful way. That might mean an email now and then, or a suggestion for a coffee, or an invitation to a social event. Whatever the case, in time, you will become a resource to them, and vice versa, and that is simply the flow of life.

Key Takeaways:

- ➢ The character you project will reflect on the person who refers you, and manners are one of the most visible embodiments of character

- First impressions are important even if you have met this person before, so do your research, be very early, pick a decent place to meet, and pay the bill
- During your meeting, eat as little as possible, be very focused on your contact, and don't be too presumptuous about getting an introduction
- Let the person you met know that you are grateful by expressing your gratitude openly and enthusiastically while departing and in follow-up email

Pre-Networking Meeting Checklist

- ☐ BEFORE MEETING DAY: Research the company and industry that you will be talking about
- ☐ Schedule meeting for at least 45 minutes
- ☐ Select a clean and professional location - coffee shop or?
- ☐ Dress professionally to make a good impression, even if you know this person well
- ☐ Arrive 15 minutes early in case your guest is early as well, and to ensure you are not late
- ☐ Make sure to pay for the coffee
- ☐ Open conversation with pleasantries, how family is doing, etc.
- ☐ Practice good eye contact and posture
- ☐ Transition to your job search, and be very specific about what kind of job you are looking for
- ☐ First seek advice, and hint occaisionally that you need some referrals
- ☐ If by the end of the conversation no introductions have been offered, you can gently ask
- ☐ Make sure to thank them generously when they do offer somebody for you to meet
- ☐ Make sure to follow up with a thank-you note withing 24 hours
- ☐ Thank them again for the introduction after you have met with that person

CHAPTER 12

Self-Awareness and Your Referral Plan

There are two important dimensions to understand about yourself that can help clarify your approach to the personal connecting process. The first is your level of expertise in the field you want to work in, and the second is your own level of personal energy in connecting with other people.

Your personal level of energy impacts how much people are drawn to you, and conveying positive energy tends to make positive impressions in several ways. First, energetic and enthusiastic individuals are seen as being more fun and interesting to be around, leading to statements like, "I enjoy working with her," or "He brings a lot to the company." Second, the impression is that people who have high external energy are more productive. The combination is the perception that they are more fun and more productive, which is the kind of personality that people are likely to hire (and refer more freely).

The degree of expertise you have in your chosen field defines the amount of value you can bring to a company. When somebody is seen as "one of the best that I've ever worked with," he or she can get very strong endorsements and tends to find new work quickly. On the other hand, when someone is new in an industry, or for whatever reason not seen as having a good level of expertise, it is harder for hiring managers to see that person in a new role, and it's more challenging for someone to decide to make a recommendation.

It would be great if we were all in the high energy/high expertise category, but that's just not the case. Many people are embarking on new industries and are looking for the chance to find meaningful work. Other people are experts at what they do, but because they are "low key," or just not very extrovert, they have a hard time selling themselves to hiring managers. The illustration on the next page may help put this point across.

Personality and Expertise Matrix

The chart above shows how different people will use different approaches to their personal meetings. Make sure you know who you are in this spectrum, and emphasize your strengths when you meet with your contacts.

Plan—Where Do You Lean?

- If you are a Magnet, one broad-based email to your network will yield big results. Include prior work associates. You are in the strongest job search position, so set your goals very high. Find your ideal job and go get it.
- If you are a Thoroughbred, the personal network outreach can yield some results, but don't be concerned, AT ALL, if it doesn't. It just means that your persona does not generate as much emotional passion in others to move you to your next job. HOWEVER, your expertise is hugely valuable, and with face-to-face meetings, you can generate excellent support and action.
- If you are a Team Player, you can get good responses from your personal outreach email, and you will get good results from your in-person meetings. For people like you, meetings in person generate lots of energy, and people want to help you.
- If you are a Development Player, you need to hit the personal meetings hard. You need to engage a greater number of people to help you generate ideas and connections. THERE IS A GREAT JOB FOR EVERYONE, and you will find yours. But, there are a few observations to consider.

For the Development Player

First, you are either a pessimist, depressed, or a realist. Nobody put you in the low energy/low expertise bucket but yourself, so let's break down the reasons behind your selection.

- The Realist:
  - You have decided to take on a new career and you realize that you still do not possess the skills required to thrive in that career. You want to learn, and you are willing to put in the work to prove that you deserve the shot

    - You are socially a bit more reserved, hence, you don't see yourself as naturally getting energy and/or giving energy from people interactions
- The Pessimist:
    - You are more of an expert than you give yourself credit for, OR
    - You are a high-energy person on the job, but you lack social confidence, so you don't give yourself credit.
- The Depressed:
    - You used to give yourself credit for being highly skilled and having high energy on the job, but for whatever reason, perhaps a very hard job search process, you have come to doubt yourself and your abilities.
    - If you have been working on the typical job search applications process, and networking without target intent, you may be depressed, pessimistic, or some combination of both.

I recommend that the people who place themselves in the Development Player bucket should start their in-person meetings with five people who know their work very well. These are the people you have worked with and have a good relationship with. In these meetings, you share with these people that you are exploring your next career moves, and you would like them to provide you with feedback. Ask them to describe what they see as your top three strengths and top three weaknesses. Ask them to provide advice based on what they know about you, and what they would recommend for a next step.

Listen carefully to the types of jobs they see you in, as this reveals their perception of your overall balance of skills. What typically happens in these meetings is that people discover that they are actually farther in the upper scale of either expertise or people energy, or both. This is important because starting with a firm grounding on one's self is essential to displaying the confidence that employers need to see when interviewing.

The Brutal Honest Truth

One of the odd parts of being part of a social world is that people are very sensitive to hurting other people's feelings. In the process of job finding, you want your connections to ignore their feelings and be brutally honest. But they won't, even if you ask them. It's too hard to hurt somebody's feelings—which is why I recommend this technique, as it helps bring the honesty forward:

1. Ask them to tell you with some degree of specificity what they see as your three greatest strengths.
2. Ask them to tell you what they see as the most important thing for you to change. Tell them that you want to hear the unvarnished truth. The next answer will be somewhat direct, but still not brutally honest.
3. Tell them that most people are thinking of something that is too hard to get across, and too hurtful, so they don't do it. But you want a job, and you want to improve, and you need to hear it.
4. Then brace yourself as you may hear things like: Your hair is just too crazy for this industry. Your eating habits are a bit offensive, mouth open, etc. You never look me in the eye when you talk. Whatever it is, you want to know.

Looking back, one of the most memorable interviews I had took place when I was eighteen and applied for a position of a ski instructor in the local mountains near Los Angeles. There were about forty people in the running for eight positions. I was being interviewed by four people at once, and I thought I had great answers to all the questions. But they came back and said, "You are on the 'maybe' list, because you didn't look us in the eye when you answered questions." They asked, "How are you going to command respect from students if you don't look them in the eye?" This knocked the air out of me, as I couldn't recall anyone ever telling me that you should look people in the eye when talking to them. I'm *sure* I was told that repeatedly during my childhood, but I blanked. I changed my eye contact behavior, perhaps staring people down a little too much, and got the ski instructor job.

The point of forcing the people you are meeting with to tell you the horrible, unvarnished truth is this: If they see a personal flaw that makes them feel uneasy, they have told themselves that they can't go too far out on a limb to make an introduction for you. However, if you get that out on the table, acknowledge the point, laugh about it, and thank them profusely, your contact opens up to the idea of an introduction tremendously. Help them be at ease, and learn something important from many of your meetings. These are the little things that can make a big difference in your referrals. Of course, use some common social sense in this process. People who know you better will be able to dig deeper into the sensitive stuff. People you are connected to through a mutual person will not share as much, unless they are extremely skilled at providing feedback or just plain assertive.

Key Takeaways:

- High-energy people who give and/or get energy from interacting with others tend to get referrals more easily
- Highly skilled people who command respect for their expertise will always have options, but may need to probe a bit more for the recommendations
- People with low skills who are either just getting started in a field or thinking of changing careers need to place a huge emphasis on meeting with people that can help them get a footing
- People who see themselves with low skills and are also mild mannered will have to work at both skill development and relationship building with in-person meetings to increase their chances of getting the right job
- Ask a series of questions to get your contact to tell you the brutal honest truth about what you need to do to be a better candidate for a job

CHAPTER 13

Your Foundation of Confidence

Job seeking is a unique part of life where even the most accomplished people can have their personal confidence shaken. Packaging yourself with résumés and cover letters and interviews is a series of steps that are designed for you to be evaluated, measured, and accepted or rejected. Very few people are accepted at every step, and each time we fail, we experience some sense of vulnerability and rejection.

So let's explore the logical reasons for you to be confident. Ultimately, confidence is a feeling, an emotion, but I believe that our emotions are driven by what we believe in our logical mind.

Understanding the Psychology of Being a Job Seeker

When you wake up in the morning and know that you need to get a job, a feeling of fear and uncertainty slaps you in the face. These feelings are driven by a human trait where it is very hard to be proactive if you do not have a finite goal in front of you. Job finding is like that—it is clear that you need to get a job. You can even set a target job goal, ideal timeframes to shoot for, but in the end, there is no clear company, date, or position that you know you are working toward. In his book, *Man's Search for Meaning,* Victor

Frankl describes the psychological state of an unemployed person as similar to that of a war prisoner:

> *"A man who could not see the end of his provisional existence was not able to aim at an ultimate goal in life. He ceased living for the future, in contrast to a man in normal life. Therefore, the whole structure of his inner life changed; signs of decay set in, which we know from other areas of life. The unemployed worker, for example, is in a similar position. His existence has become provisional and, in a certain sense, he cannot work for the future or aim at a goal. Research work done on unemployed miners suggests that they suffer from a peculiar sort of deformed time—inner time—which is a result of their unemployed state."*[5]

Frankl is bringing clarity to the phenomenon that has two dimensions. The first is the sense of aimlessness a job seeker feels when setting out to find a job—aimlessness because of the lack of a concrete finish line in both the time and the company. The second is this idea of "inner time," where one day can feel like an entire week, which is an outcropping of the clash between the urgency of finding a job and the sense of aimlessness in getting it. When you are in the space if inner time, the pain of your current situation is so present that time passes excruciatingly slowly, which does not help your productivity. You can think of this "inner time" as the opposite of being in the "flow."

This, therefore, is what leads to job search paralysis and, in some cases, causes people to feel some level of depression and loss of confidence. But there is a way out of this, and it consists of two parts:

> First, having an understanding of how the human mind normally reacts to the unemployed situation gives you the ability to see it for what it is and move beyond that. Armed with this information, you can recognize this state of mind

5 *Man's Search for Meaning*, Victor E. Frankl, page 70

and set your sights at overcoming it, rather than being caught up in the inertia.

Second, by creating a comprehensive job search plan and executing it every day, you create concrete near-term goals that are achievable, giving you a sense of greater purpose. By following the guidelines in this book, for example, you can stay busy every day, not doing hard work, but doing the right things that bring you energy, and by doing so, you are achieving your near-term goals from which your ideal job will emerge.

This example of comparing the unemployed person's state of mind to that of a prisoner may seem a bit drastic, but understanding the way through a feeling of aimlessness is a big boost to your confidence.

Reframe Your View of the Concept of Intelligence

After working with possibly some of the smartest people in the world at the Microsoft Corporation, I had a moment of clarity with regards to the meaning of intelligence. The question I was continually baffled by was this: "Why is it that so many people with genius IQs and intimidating academic accomplishments so frequently struggle in business?"

The answer came to me when I read an article about a concept that changed the way I see the world. The article was about Triarchic Intelligence,[6] which defines three types of intelligence. I have applied my own variation on the concept with these definitions:

- Analytic Intelligence: The ability to learn and analyze vast amounts of information. This is the classic definition of

6 The concept of Triarchic Intelligence is credited to Robert Sternberg

intelligence as defined by IQ tests, SAT tests, and our school system in general.
- Creative Intelligence: The ability to create, invent, build, and shape. Given the same information and a challenge to create something new from that information, some people can create spectacular things, while others can't.
- Intuitive Intelligence: The ability to see and understand how things work when there is no clear map or instruction manual. This includes the ability to understand people and persuade them, as well as the ability to understand how organizations or mechanical things work together.

For me, this was a fascinating discovery. Rather than defining creativity as a talent some people have and some don't, it's seen as a form of intelligence. Understanding that the ability to read people and adapt to their styles in order to forge better relationships is a form of intelligence rather than just a personality trait, and is a huge shift in both how people are defined and in how we can see ourselves.

We go through our entire school years with an enormous focus on the analytic learning side of life. Why? It's concrete, it's measurable, and it helps to shape the core talents that define the foundation of most jobs. I have come to believe, however, that this is one of the most destructive elements that exist when it relates to shaping and defining each person's sense of value and worth. That's because some kids are always at the top of the curve by virtue of some combination of hard work and analytic intelligence, but most aren't. Therefore, if you go through school knowing that you are second best, or lower, you define your potential, your aspirations, and your very being in these terms.

I think that this is a major failing of our system, because work is so essential to the structure of life and how we feel about ourselves, and a person's potential for work success is defined by the three elements of intelligence, not just analytic. In a harsh way, this means that many people who have enormous potential to accomplish spectacular things emerge from the education system with little sense of this potential. What a spectacular failure of our culture and our approach to raising kids!

Instead, we should share the understanding that each person has a combination of analytic, creative, and intuitive intelligence that is entirely unique. It is as unique as a fingerprint. Nobody in the world can do what you can do, the way you do it.

I once met a senior executive search recruiter who shared with me that "there is a perfect job for everyone." I like to see the world in this light. It's a foundation of why I advise people to look at work as a life journey towards your ideal job. In this context, your ideal job is often where your unique talents are valued, applied, challenged, stretched, and needed. In an environment where you have these opportunities, as I shared at the beginning of the book, you will be excited to get up to go to work. You will find the opportunity to immerse yourself so deeply in your projects that you lose track of time. And you will create spectacular things.

So why I did I choose to include this topic in this section? Because while you are job hunting, there is no better thing for you to fully grasp and understand than the absolute certainty that:

- You have unique value to offer
- There is a perfect job for everybody

Armed with this knowledge, your job search becomes a mission to get to that place.

From my own evolution, once I understood the three types of intelligence, it became clear that success in business is more closely linked to creative and intuitive intelligence than it is to analytic intelligence. Success in the professions such as medicine, law, sciences, and engineering is more related to analytic intelligence. I now enjoy seeing people through this lens and, as a manager of people, it helps arm me with the ability to tailor projects and responsibilities to help people put their most unique talents to work.

Why Being Fired Should Not Dent Your Confidence

If you are one of the people who have been laid-off or just plain fired, the typical reaction is to feel a blow to the ego. We all want to be appreciated, respected, and valued for the contributions that we make. Getting fired makes us wonder what we did wrong, what could have been better, and we often feel a sense of injustice that other people who should have been let go were kept.

Although we explored the mind of the manager in Chapter 4, we need to go there again. Typically, there are two main reasons why people are let go: 1) they don't get along with their manager or the team, and 2) they are not perceived as capable of doing the job. What is interesting is that the two are often blended and confused, as a manager cannot go to the HR department and start the process of a termination just on the basis that they don't "like" the employee. They need to document in some detail the failures of that employee to do the required work. On the flipside, it's rare for a manager to like someone who does not deliver, as that person becomes a source of frustration.

So, if you were fired, the takeaway for you should be that you were simply not a good fit. That's it. It has nothing to do with your worth. It has nothing to do with your potential in the future. Take it as a learning experience about what you don't want to do, about where your ideal job is not, and move on.

With eyes wide open, you can reset on your lifetime journey to find and re-find your ideal job. Since I am showing you how job finding can be easy, take it as an opportunity to clearly define your balance of the three types of intelligences, your interests, and the areas you are most passionate about. Armed with that information, you can probe the people you meet with in greater detail. You will be effortlessly asking the kinds of questions and leading discussions that help shape a picture of what your ideal job could be. They can introduce you to new types of jobs and careers if they have clear understanding of what you do and don't want. In this constant discovery process, you will uncover new and relevant options along the way and you will be energized as you see with greater clarity what it is that you need to find to call it your ideal job.

Work Structures Life

If you are currently not working, you are in a bit of a free-form daily schedule, which often means sleeping in, casual personal commitments to getting projects done, interruptions by spouses and friends asking you to do chores, and distractions of exercise and entertainment. One of the problems with being in this mode is that it lacks the structure that work provides to create urgency, purposefulness, and results. You are not in an environment where you are needed for the productivity of the organization, and most people miss the interaction of peers and the social pace of the workplace.

Bill Clinton once said that "Work organizes life. It gives structure and discipline to life," and since hearing this and thinking about it, I see work through a completely different lens. Work provides a human being an opportunity for the social integration, acceptance, and validation that we all need. By following the steps in this book, while you are prospecting you won't need to do a lot, but you do need to get your basics done early in your search process, and make sure that you keep your in-person meetings coming. As soon as you have job interviews lined up, that is the point for you to see your job search as a full-time job. Research the companies and seek out internal referrals. You should get up at the same time you normally would for work, get dressed in professional work attire, have a workspace, whether a home office or elsewhere, get to that workspace and focus.

A Great Plan Builds Confidence

Strategy. Plan. Action. Any activity that is going to result in a predictable outcome needs all three.

Strategy

The strategy is where you apply your goal to the situation around you, and you define those areas of opportunity that you can take advantage of. Your strategy is the grand design of how you are going to apply your energy, your mind, and your passion, and the result of that grand well-executed design is success. The strategy is often tied to a few elements of insight that re-frame how you have previously seen the world. The insight of a well-constructed job search is the essence that people want to help, and that they are flattered if you ask.

Your strategy for your job search should be to focus on the huge potential of personal connections. You should aim to meet with people you have in your direct or indirect personal network, people who you previously may have never considered, but because of your insight, you know now that you must. You should not be satisfied with meeting just one or two, but dozens and dozens of people.

Plan

The plan is the part that defines what you are going to do and when, so the opportunity you have uncovered in your strategy can reasonably be attained. It is the part that you review every day, every morning, and it is well thought through in advance. The plan is your promise to yourself that you are going to allocate the priority of your time to the things that matter the most. It is what allows you to get up in the morning when the future seems doubtful and bleak, and look at yourself in the mirror and realize that you are on a path to a better place. It is what enables you to be confident that you are on track and everything will be okay. When you have an insight, a strategy and a plan, you feel the power of clarity and positive destiny all the way from your feet to your soul.

Your plan for your job search should be to get the computer work behind you by following the basics in this book, and then spend your time every day initiating, scheduling, and going on meetings, always making sure that you follow up. The people you will meet are a combination of your closest friends, your most distant and powerful personal connections, and everybody in between. If you are alive and living on planet Earth, you will have dozens and dozens of people to meet with. It is not until you go through the exercise of working through the different people that you know or contacts from your friends and family that you can even comprehend the number of possibilities. Most people have hundreds of people they know that they could potentially meet with to discuss their job search. Start with some of your closest friends and follow the action plan. Then move to the most influential people you can see in your network. And seek out those people who need help with their job! Coach and mentor.

Action

The action part starts every morning after you have reviewed your plan. If your plan is well executed, you will have two or even three meetings per day already scheduled, and will be initiating as many new ones. You will also be doing all the scheduling and following up to keep that pace going. Action is that process where you get into a rhythm of preparing for a meeting, being early for a meeting, handling the meeting well, and doing it again. Action is the process where the work you do every day is following your plan, and you are rewarded at the end of every day with the fruits of your work. Progress is palpable. You can feel it in your toes.

Your action is a matter of how seriously you are taking your job search. If you are committed to turning your strategy and your plan into a reality, you will attack your action items quickly and aggressively.

The action of meeting with people is so energizing and positive that you will find that it is easy.

It is easy to take action that delivers meaningful results . . . . Sounds crazy? It's not; it's quite real. You just need the right insight, the right strategy, and the right plan. You now have it.

Tenacity, Activity, and Achievement

Do not mistake activity for achievement. Many people do busy-work and feel that since they are working hard, they are achieving. This is only the case if it yields results. So make sure that you are meeting your goals of personal meetings, personal outreach, follow-up notes, etc. Hold yourself to a high-quantitative measurement of completing the things that need to be done for the job opportunity to happen.

Tenacity is the single most common trait of successful people, more so than any of the three intelligences, and more so than a specific profession. Never give up. Quitters never win, and winners never quit.

Key Takeaways:

- Know *your* unique intelligence by assessing your balance of analytic, creative, and intuitive intelligence as objectively as you can
- Know that there is a perfect job for everyone
- If you were let go from your prior company, it was because your personality and work style were not a good "fit" with your boss and/or the company, not because of any deficiency in your potential
- Define and create your strategy and your plan, then take action every day
- Make sure that you are producing results, not busy-work, and be tenacious

CHAPTER 14

Create Your Job Search Dream Team

Let's revisit the most important lesson for any job seeker—successful people want to help. If you take that as the starting point for a strategy on how to maximize your chances for a great job, then you will consider the following questions: 1) Which people I should contact and, 2) how often can I engage them? The answers to these questions provide the framework for how to set up your job search dream team. Your dream team includes ten to twenty-five people who are more senior than you are in business, as well as connected and interested in seeing you succeed in your job search.

I suggest that your dream team should include the following groups:

a. Your five most accomplished friends—they have ideas and connections, and successful people just know how to make things happen
b. Your five most connected friends—some people are just natural connectors and relationship builders. They get a charge out of putting people together for mutual benefit
c. Five to ten of the most senior executives you have in your personal network. These are some of the most accomplished people on your list from Chapter 10.

d. Five-to-ten prior work associates who are either more senior than you are or extremely well connected. These should all be people you had a good working relationship with, such as former supervisors.

This group of people can be identified as a dream team, because this combination is certain to give you feedback that will help you improve. They will give you ideas on how to leverage your strengths, and they will connect you with people who can help your career. It is not different from all the people we noted in Chapter 10, but it is a sub-segment where you identify how these most influential people can help you more specifically. These are the people who will most likely help you find the right results.

Tips for the Creation of the Dream Team

One of the greatest mistakes people make is failing to follow up meetings with influential people correctly. After the meeting, many people forget to send a thank-you note. Some forget to send a status update, and fail to send a got-a-job note with new contact information. These people are like hit-and-run acquaintances who get what they can from you and disappear.

In my research with mid- and senior-level executives, I was surprised to learn that about half of all the people who call and ask for a meeting and an introduction never send a thank-you note. This does not impress the people who were asked. In fact, although most executives just shrug it off as a sign of the times, they see people who ask for help and can't be bothered to send a thank-you note as plain rude and unappreciative.

The reality is that this is one of the most "binary" dynamics in business. Binary is the cool Silicon Valley word for black or white. In this case, if you send a thank-you note and the right follow-up notes then you create tremendous goodwill, whereas you will generate resentment otherwise.

But what we are talking about is not just the good or bad will; it is about building relationships and trust. If you follow the basics of professional courtesy, you will send these messages to the people you have met:

- Thank-you note for the meeting
- Thank-you note after meeting with the person your contact referred you to
- Status updates every few weeks when there is news
- Thank-you note with the "got a job" announcement

An amazing thing happens when you follow the basic elements of courtesy: your call is welcome when you reach out a few weeks later. I recommend that, after meeting with the connections you were offered, you send a note to the original contact acknowledging the meeting with the referred person, and then reach back with a call or an email.

By sending the right thank-you notes, you have passed an unwritten test. You can be trusted to be respectful, courteous, and professional with contacts. This demonstrates respect to the person who made the introduction and strengthens the relationship. By passing the unwritten test, you are confirming to the person that he or she can trust you with his or her personal network. When you reach out, you do so with another request. Something like this:

> *Mary, my search continues to go well and I have several interesting discussions in progress, but I could still use a few good connections. Is there anyone else you can think of to introduce me to?*

Very often, your contact will find another name to introduce you to, and it is not uncommon for this introduction to be *more* influential than the first.

Some points are so important that they are worth restating: After you demonstrate exceptional business courtesy, your request for an additional contact is frequently met with a more influential person than the first contact. Why? Well, the people you are meeting with do want to help you, but they have to weigh the burden of the introduction to another person in the process. There is risk in sending you to their most valued connections, and until you give them a reason to believe that you are trustworthy with that risk, they will typically make the first introduction to a good, but perhaps not great connection.

As you build your dream team, they will empower you, embolden you, connect you, and put you in a position to do great things. Always offer to help them in any way you can. You never know when they might have a similar need where you can help.

Key Takeaways:

- Define your dream team in groups of people from successful friends, to senior executive connections, to prior business associates
- Good follow-up communication after meetings helps build trust and opens the door for future requests
- Poor follow-up habits erode relationships and significantly reduce your ability to get follow-on referrals
- Very often, your contacts are more willing to introduce you to more influential people once you have demonstrated excellent professional courtesy through your communications

CHAPTER 15

Helping Other Job Seekers

Now that you know how to make job finding easy and energizing, and you understand a bit about the importance of setting your goals and creating your job search plan to find your ideal job, you have the knowledge and the potential to help other job seekers.

I recommend that you meet with two job seekers every week. Fitting this into a ten-per-week meeting schedule with your core networking may feel like a lot, but it is well worth it for many reasons.

First, by meeting with other people with the intent to help them with their job search, you are providing very real and needed assistance. You are giving, and it feels good to give generously. Three things happen when you do this: as you are adding value to somebody else's life, you are benefiting from your own sense of generosity and, perhaps most importantly, by experiencing the feeling of helping others, you more deeply understand why it's okay for you to reach out and ask for meetings. This is not a secondary thought. The inner confidence you get from asking for meetings through your personal network helps open your mind, frees you from your fears, and uncovers huge opportunities.

Second, being the leader and mentor gives you more confidence. Watching the reactions of others as they look to you as the expert removes doubt from your mind and actually helps you visualize yourself in a more assertive and confident view.

Third, reviewing the key elements of job search with others reinforces your own awareness of the role that each part plays. There is a saying that in order to truly be an expert at something, you should learn it well enough to be able to teach it. The review and the reinforcement will improve your own execution of the most important steps.

Fourth, building and strengthening relationships with others almost always has some added element of value. You never know if one of the people you are helping might have a personal connection to someone who can make the difference in your career. Moreover, after you provide someone with the tools to make their world better, they will go out of their way to help you in any way they can.

Lastly, meeting with people you are going to help is a completely stress-free process. You can let your hair down, exhale, and just relax. People need to laugh every day, and the more time you spend as a mentor and coach, the more time you see with great clarity that the relationship and the enjoyment you can get from the interactions are essential elements of connecting with others.

The job search approach defined in this book is all about getting computers out of the way and letting the power and generosity of humanity bring opportunities and ideas forward in a way that makes computer approaches seem irrelevant. You may find the study of the human dynamics of job finding interesting. You may read more and more about it, and you may even find that you develop theories of your own. We are simply systematically presenting the steps needed to bring jobs forward and examining the core of what humans bring to the process so that you can understand it better. Behavioral search and hiring.

Remember, when you offer to help somebody, you might need to initiate the process. You can open people's minds by asking them how many people they have met with. Ask if they know the first rule of careers (nobody is successful alone). Get used to the idea that if you want to be part of the working world, you must be a part of the people-helping-people cycle. HELPING others is just part of the cycle. Successful people know this.

Key Takeaways:

- You have the knowledge to make a difference in other job seekers' lives, and it feels good to help other people
- Helping others helps to ingrain in you the acceptability of asking others to meet with you
- Helping others builds your confidence, brings clarity to your own plan, and potentially creates some unexpected introductions

CHAPTER 16

Mentoring

The formalization of a relationship based on the win-win of the advisor/advisee is called mentoring. In talking with executives at the highest levels and with young college grads, I have found that mentoring is not well understood. Mentoring in its simplest form is rarely practiced. In my view, a mentor is someone who meets with you every few months for a reflective and non-threatening conversation about your job, your career, your skills, and your perspectives about business.

The mentor's job is the easiest in the world; all he or she needs to do is just show up. They already know an enormous amount about what it takes to succeed. When you share your situation, they react and respond intuitively. People love to talk, give advice, and be sought out for their expertise. In time, the mentor relationship can evolve to recommendations, meaningful referrals, and more. The point of mentoring is that, apart from general career discussions, you rarely know in advance what the topic is. These are not problem-resolution relationships, although at times they can be. Think of it like "*The Seinfeld Show*" of business. What's this about? It's about nothing, which is to say, it's about those things that happen to us in our daily lives that we try to understand, laugh at, and learn from.

If you are a mid-level to senior executive and you find a junior person who shows great potential and exudes positive chemistry, take a step to meet with them and offer to be a mentor. Teach them about what a mentor is and does.

All people, at all levels, should find their mentors. Two is a good number, although some might seek more. Start with a coffee, and if you sense positive chemistry with that person, then make a specific request for them to be a mentor. You will likely have to clarify your expectations of that mentorship. You can say something like, "We can meet every few months for coffee, and I will share with you my stories, my decisions, my concerns, etc. In return, I would like you to share with me your reactions and perspectives." I say this because when I was in my role as Director of Worldwide Marketing at Pepsi-Cola International, a new marketing person invited me to lunch and asked me to be a mentor. I had no idea what that meant. How much work? How much time? What if I didn't have the right expertise?

In interviewing middle and senior level executives, I have learned that very few have been asked to be mentors, and very few younger people have asked others to be mentors. This is one of those things that many people seem to think of as a good idea, but they don't get around to it. Most people don't have enough perspective to understand that successful people have hundreds of tips about how to be successful. They have experience with complex scenarios with company politics, project work, leveraging strengths, self-promotion, industry insight . . . . The list goes on and on.

I find that people who rise quickly are more active in seeking mentors. They have learned that the key to success is through connecting with people, i.e., building the relationships that provide the insight they need. When you select the right mentors, you can learn a lifetime of secrets of success in just a few lunches and coffee meetings. If you are truly on a mission to find your ideal job, you will want to become a voracious learner from the people who are living that role you aspire to be in. In order to allocate time to this, however, you have to understand that you are not aware of most of the things that can lead to your success, and you don't know what you don't know. The wrong mindset is to say to yourself, "I can't think of why I would meet with this person. I can't think of anything he or she might tell me, so why meet?" This is the thinking of a person who works his or her fingers to the bone for a lifetime, wondering all the while why more opportunities failed to materialize.

I would suggest that you not try to select people who could be your potential mentors until you have had five or ten meetings with different influential people. After that kind of exposure, the people you want to be your mentors will become obvious. A few of them will seem to have an outlook and a humor that you deeply admire. A few will have an admirable success path. A few will have a reciprocal interest in you that you can sense, and one or two will have the right combination of all of the above.

My story

My first mentor was my high school photography teacher, Mark Effle. I didn't know it then, but when a mentee succeeds, the mentor takes great pride. When I was fourteen years old, I became fascinated with photography and dived in. The money I had saved for that motorcycle my dad never bought me went to a good camera instead, and I spent a great deal of my four years of high school in photo shop, shooting motorcycles, cars, and girls. At least three days a week, I stayed very late after school, and every week Mr. Effle would keep the lab open for me. When I was sixteen, instead of buying a car, I kept spending money on cameras, film, and experimenting with new techniques.

Mr. Effle would not only investigate new techniques with me, but he would give me a ride home. He devoted a lot of time just to me, as not that many kids wanted to stay late. As a senior, I was getting a lot of recognition for my work and won several national contests, which led to scholarships from both Nikon and Kodak. The local newspaper did a feature article on me and listed the various awards.

Well, photography got me through college, as I worked full time in a lab and shooting weddings. Since I went into marketing, my photo background has always been helpful in the creation of imagery, and at Pepsi-Cola, in particular, image marketing was everything. I didn't visit my hometown often, and almost never mid-week, but several times over the years after leaving high school I thought of stopping in to see Mr. Effle. It wasn't until twenty-five years after my high school graduation that I made my way to the school when class was in session. I strolled into the photo shop, which looked eerily similar to the way it was twenty-five years earlier, and greeted my old friend and mentor. What a nice feeling it was to share the stories of the time in-between, and thank him for his time and interest in me.

As we were wrapping up our conversation, as he had another class about to start, he said he had something to show me. We walked over to his desk, he opened the top right drawer, pulled out a plastic pencil tray, and from under the tray, he picked up a newspaper clipping and handed it to me. It was the article about me from 1976! He looked at me and said, "I never had another one like you."

It was quite a "Hallmark" moment for me, for us, and I realized then that for all the time he spent with me, he took great satisfaction from my successes. Of course.

Overall, the hardest part of the mentoring process is asking people for introductory meetings. Yet, there is nothing hard about this. Once you have identified a few people that you would like to mentor you, it should feel pretty natural to ask for that mentorship. This becomes even easier if you keep repeating to yourself the most important lesson: People want to help, and they are flattered when you ask. So do it! You will see that this is one of the most powerful things you can do for your career, and after you do it, you will agree . . . that it was easy. Powerful and easy, my favorite combination.

Just as we suggested that you proactively help other job seekers with their pursuits, it is equally important and rewarding to identify a few people for you to mentor. Every year, a new crop of kids become adults and are thrown into the world of work, and every single one of them is in need of help and direction. They don't all know it, but they are. Some come from accomplished families and have grown up with ample opportunities for coaching, but they still don't know much. Some come from less successful families, and hence with fewer perspectives about the secrets of success. Help a few kids with advice, and you will be rewarded with satisfaction in many ways.

Key Takeaways:

- Everybody needs mentors if they want to be on a fast track to jobs and career success
- Select mentors whom you admire and have good chemistry with
- Be a mentor to a young person that you feel has great potential

The mindset of the person who gets on the fast track to their ideal job

I have decided to never settle for a job that I am not excited about, and not stay in a job out of fear of what might come next. Since no one can be successful alone, I have promised myself to frequently ask advice from influential personal connections. And although it makes me feel vulnerable, I remind myself that a request for advice is seen by others as confidence and strength. So I commit to ask for advice about career perspectives, résumé feedback, and job leads. I boldly reach up to the most powerful people who know me or know of me, grounded in the truth that successful people want to help, and they are flattered when I ask. I take a deep breath and remind myself of this again, they are flattered when I ask. I recall how good I feel following these meetings, and their smiles convince me that they felt the same. I know that this is the essential social fabric of humanity, and I only need to offer a formal thank you in exchange - the gesture with the benefit of building enduring relationships and not eroding them. I move forward everyday with relentless tenacity because I know that as long as I am aware of my ignorance, and at the same time confident in my ability to learn, I will succeed.

SECTION IV

Special Situations

When Extra Creativity Is Required, Invoke the Merlin Factor[7]

Many people are going to find their best opportunities in unexpected places, and in ways that are not immediately apparent today. To help prepare you for setting a course into uncertainty and feeling good about it, the Merlin Factor is magic. It blends an understanding of the essence of how the human mind generates creative thinking with the idea of setting a hard and worthy goal.

Studies on creativity show that creativity happens when the subconscious mind is engaged and works in your favor. This is the same process that you are trying to spur in the people you meet with in your one-on-one meetings. It works this way: you first task yourself with a serious problem; you immerse yourself in the complexities

---

7 *The Merlin Factor: Leadership and Strategic Intent,* by Charles E. Smith, Business Strategy Review, Volume 5, Issue 1, 1994, published by Oxford University Press

and various dimensions of the problem, and work hard to identify options; then you put it out of your mind. When you release your conscious mind from the problem, your subconscious mind is still working on it.

Some people find answers in minutes, "seemingly" out of nowhere. Other people task themselves with the problem before bed, and answers pop into their minds at 3:00 a.m. That's how it works for me. I am constantly getting out of bed at 3:00 or 4:00 a.m. to jot down ideas. My mother always told me to put a pad of paper and a pencil on the nightstand next to my bed. Regardless of how it happens, if you blend the right amount of urgency and immersion into a problem, perhaps even revisiting it several times a day, creative answers will appear.

Now imagine what happens when you set a big goal. A big goal is often made up of many smaller goals, or smaller problems that need to be solved in order to reach that big goal. You frame the goal in your mind in a way that helps you see the first step or first problem that needs to be solved. As you apply the elements of creativity to that problem, you will find a creative answer, upon which the next challenge in the process becomes clear.

The visual example is that you are building a bridge from where you are to that big goal. You don't have a blueprint that specifies each step to get there. You are not even sure what the steps will be, or what hurdles will need to be overcome. The parts that are unknown are daunting, and many people won't set out to achieve a goal unless they have these steps defined.

The application of the Merlin Factor is the belief, the understanding, that with urgency, immersion and time, you can arrive at that goal. You don't have to be able to see all the steps now, because it's impossible to see today the steps of opportunity or challenge that the future holds. It is impossible now to know what your creative mind will come up with. It is the confidence in your ability to solve problems and the pure desire to reach a goal that keeps you going.

It is called the Merlin Factor, because once you understand the principle of setting and working towards a goal, and you allow creativity and an evolving situation to unfold, a magical result appears along the way.

CHAPTER 17

Job Searching for the Currently Employed

This book is titled *The Fast Track to Your Ideal Job* for the specific reason of including currently employed people in the context. I have tailored much of the book to the unemployed, but the foundation is the same for the employed.

The fact is, and probably always will be, that it is far easier to get a job if you currently have a job. As an employed person, you have great advantage in this process, as you don't urgently need a job. The giant elephant in the room, however, is that job searching while you are currently employed poses a certain risk. The risk is that your current employer will find out about your search. It might be noticed that you are away from the office too often, disrupting the rhythm of work and your team around you. The repercussions of being discovered by your current employer vary from getting a raise to being summarily fired.

The risk of being fired makes people very nervous, and I think prevents many from taking the action that they know they want to take. So, in this chapter I'll review the best balance of things for you to do to architect a nearly risk-free search. The process will be energizing, fun, and extend and build relationships that you can build on for your entire career.

Here's the slightly adapted approach:

A personal email: Don't ever write anything in a company email that relates to job changing. Companies have sophisticated ways of looking at your emails to find the indications of job changing. This is legal, although I consider it an invasion of your privacy. Because of this:

- Do not give your work email to anyone who may send you a note about a job.
- Do not put your work email on your résumé
- Your personal email needs to look professional. Simply use your first name then last name through Gmail: Mary.Smythwalten@gmail.com. In no case should you use an email that does not have your name, as personal emails such as pricklypear8@aol.com paint a picture of somebody who is not serious.

Career sites: No reason to be on them. It's too easy for your company to see that you have a current résumé posted, and there is only one reason to have a current résumé posted on a job site like Monster, CareerBuilder, Dice, etc.

LinkedIn: Remember that LinkedIn is the primary place that recruiters look for employed people to recruit, so have a very well-written summary of your career and your background on LinkedIn.

- You don't need to include a résumé, as résumés present you as an active job seeker, and some recruiters shy away from that. Moreover, posting a current résumé is a signal to your company that you are keeping your eyes wide open for new opportunities.
- When considering adding people to LinkedIn that you would like to meet with, it is far better to send them an

email and ask for a meeting before asking to connect on LinkedIn. This is because of a bit of an insidious dimension of LinkedIn that lessens the quality of the personal outreach if that outreach starts with a link request. The receiver sees the connection request and may or may not accept it, depending on his or her level of engagement with LinkedIn. When you follow with a request to meet, the impression is that you only asked for the LinkedIn connection because you wanted something from that person and you couldn't be bothered to make much of a personal effort, so you took the LinkedIn shortcut. Far better from a relationship-building perspective to call or send an email, have the meeting, then ask for the LinkedIn connection.

- Make your personal email available

Recruiting Firms: Make sure that you send a well-written, updated résumé to the recruiting firms searching for positions like yours. Depending on your level, there are different target recruiters:

- Entry level to Manager: It's a good idea to connect with the staffing agencies that handle roles beyond clerical. Adecco and Robert Half and other companies of that caliber often have full-time assignments and are always looking for good people. You can connect with one of these firms and in many cases meet somebody at a local office.
- For people looking for director level to GM positions, the contingency recruiters in your area who specialize in your field may number as many as forty to eighty.
- For people from GM to VP and above, the executive search firms have many roles, and it is essential to get your résumé to the right firms. Depending on your profession, this could mean as many as 60 to 600 firms.

When you send your résumé to these companies, include a brief cover note that includes your most recent companies, titles, and your qualifications.

Personal Network Outreach: We don't recommend sending out too many personal network outreach emails because you just don't know who will receive them and possibly forward on. It is hard to put something innocuous in an email that both asks for a job connection and at the same time does not look like you are actively looking. If you are not so concerned about whether your employer discovers your search intent, then send more broadly.

Close Friend Outreach: Similarly, we don't recommend the close friend endorsement outreach, as it is quite hard to make it innocuous.

Meeting with People in Person: Bingo, this is the key focus area for you. You adapt your meeting request to be innocuous. Instead of, "I'd like to meet with you to discuss career options," it is slightly adapted to read, "I'd like to meet with you to talk about my long-term career goals." That email request, even in the hands of your immediate supervisor, only means that you are a career-oriented person.

In short, I recommend executing the exact steps in Section III of this book. You should focus on meeting with people in person, reaching up to senior and influential people, meeting with people who need jobs, and following up well. Since you are employed full time, you might not be able to find time to schedule ten meetings per week, but you can easily fit in four or five. And since you are employed, you will feel excellent momentum as referrals will come more easily.

When You Get an Interview: Care must be taken when you do get the opportunity to interview for another company. The world is a small place when it comes to people who know people, and it is not unusual for somebody to recognize you, email a friend who knows a friend, etc. To avoid potential problems, I recommend discussing your desire for confidentiality with the company you are going to interview with, and make every effort to arrange a meeting outside the office. I was in this situation on a job a few years ago; when I asked to meet outside the office, the company insisted that there was no confidentiality problem. This was for a CMO position, and the meetings were with the executive staff. Despite my request for confidentiality, people at my office said they knew I was interviewing at the other company before I even returned from the interview!

This is a rather extreme case, of course, but I do think that if a company is truly interested, you can make some arrangements for at least the first round of interviews to be highly discreet.

Key Takeaways:

- Currently employed people can find an ideal job by executing a stealth search using the strategies in this book
- Every step applies except the personal network outreach, the closest friend outreach, and the career sites
- Meeting in person with people using long-term career planning as a pretext is innocuous and clear at the same time

CHAPTER 18

Long-Term Unemployed

People who have been out of work for eight, twelve, or eighteen months or more, have to be aware of additional considerations in their search. The stigma you feel and the stigma that others will sense is real but not insurmountable, and you do want to have a strategy for approaching it.

First, let's examine the reasons for your unemployment. Some people take time off because they want a break, while other people have been looking for or wanting a job and just have not been able to find one.

The good news is that every step in this book applies regardless of length of time since you left your last job. I suggest that unemployed people get very aggressive following each step.

Inside the Mind of the Hiring Manager

The best way to overcome the stigma of being out of work for a long time is through people you know or some kind of personal connection. These people will give you the most support and help you with advice and introductions. Per our discussion in Chapter 4, getting to the hiring managers through some kind of personal connection gives you the benefit of the doubt.

You need to have the story about why you have been out of work well thought through. It is important that you take responsibility and not give answers like, "There just aren't any jobs." From the eyes of the employer, that's the wrong answer, as even in times of high unemployment hiring managers are still feeling that it is hard to find good people to hire. *Even in times of high unemployment, there are still jobs in the market.* The idea that you believe there are no jobs when the hiring manager feels there are not enough good people makes him/her think that you must NOT be one of the good people. Don't paint that picture for him or her.

Instead, share that you have not found the right fit for your skills, that you have been learning more about how to go about finding a job, that you have been acquiring new skills, and that you are confident that the right job will come. Share that you are excited to find the right job and that you enjoy working hard to make a difference. Find your true blend of the concepts above or add more.

A Double Focus on the Personal Connections

I said it above, and I'll say it again. From the perspective of getting an interview and the difficulty of the interview, connecting with people you know and people who can give you a strong referral is by far the most effective way to get a hiring manager to overlook the time that you have been unemployed. Yes, it is also the priority no matter how long you have been out of work, but it is even more important for people with a considerable gap in their résumé.

In order to increase the chances of finding work, prepare a very thorough list of people you know and ask them for in-person meetings. You will want to re-read Chapters 10, 11, 12, and 13 and focus on getting the meetings organized. You have far more connections and potential meetings than you know. Even if you have already reached out to people, you need to clarify your personal job goals, outline your skills, and ask for the in-person meetings.

Ask, ask, ask. Focus on referrals from every meeting, but know that you won't get referrals every time. Ask for advice to improve your résumé.

As you make your way through these meetings, you will be more and more energized. Then you need to view your connections as your Job Search Dream Team (Chapter 14). You'll naturally have better chemistry with a few, and you should ask those people to be your mentors. As you understand all these principles better and better, you will become valuable to other job seekers. So a huge part of your confidence boost, your outlook, and your opportunities will come from helping other job seekers understand these job search fundamentals.

Offer to Work on Contract as a Trial Period

One of the easiest things to do for a company is to bring somebody on in a contract position as a trial run. It is becoming common among companies to do this, and yet it is not necessarily what a hiring manager thinks of when interviewing. The hiring manager is trying to solve a long-term problem: Who is going to fill this role? Who is going to "own" this position and solve the problems that this position addresses? For most hiring managers, a contract person in that role with the possibility that the person won't work out and the hiring process would have to start again is not optimal.

But finding a perfect candidate from an interview is not easy. In that light, the suggestion that you would be happy to work on contract might open the hiring manager's mind. This is particularly true if you have a personal connection to the hiring manager, even if your skill fit is not exactly what they are looking for. It allows the hiring manager to feel that he is doing a good thing to help his contact, you, and solve the resource gap of the position. This is also a smart option for you, as both you and the company can have time to decide if there is a good fit.

Key Takeaways:

- Long-term unemployment does have a stigma to it, and you need to look to your personal network for the power of leveraged trust that helps people overlook that stigma
- Know your strengths and your goals well, so that you can arm your connections with clarity of the kinds of companies to introduce you to
- Identify a few people to be your mentors—spend more time with them for more direction
- Do not tell hiring companies that you have been out of work "because there are no jobs"
- Offering to work on contract is an excellent way to get a chance to demonstrate your skills and work ethics, and it helps you both decide if there is a good fit.

CHAPTER 19

Over Fifty

When people are over fifty, they are perceived as out of touch with the modern world. The twenty-somethings see them as grandparent-like, the thirty-somethings see them as parent-like, and the forty-somethings see them as the people who recently retired from the company.

The challenge of the over-fifty person is that corporations have dramatically fewer positions in each level up the corporate pyramid. Add to that a desire to promote high-potential junior managers combined with constant budget scrutiny, and the result is that there are very few people over fifty in many larger companies. There is also a general perception that the people over fifty don't contribute with the same intellectual energy as their younger counterparts. The combination of all of the above makes up the painful reality that people over fifty have a harder time finding their place in the job market and the workplace.

As you think about the different types of jobs to target, you will run into the challenge that while larger companies have a more robust promotion and "up or out" cycle, they also tend to pay at substantially higher levels than smaller companies. Smaller companies have the benefit of being more personal, with more trust-based decision making, particularly if the person in charge is respected by the CEO. As a result, many people in their fifties find longevity and satisfaction working in smaller companies, as they enjoy the culture and versatility of work their role entails, without the political pressures of a large company. Another common avenue for more mature workers is consulting, although this takes a certain amount of ability to define a clear value that you can deliver, and the ability to close the sale on new business. Some people decide to start a business, which requires an entirely higher level of personal commitment and sacrifice.

The Right Place at the Right Time

When it comes to finding permanent employment, you need to be in the right place at the right time, but how do you make sure that you recognize and capitalize on such coincidental opportunities? Following the career site, recruiter, personal outreach, and networking elements presented in this book combine to create the most effective way to do this. The scope of your value and the potential for people to help are hard to express.

Personal Network Outreach

As with everything important in your life, you want to operate from a position of strength. Your strength is that you have met thousands of people through your years in business. If you want an outstanding job, your ideal job, you will want to leverage these connections. When you add up all the people in your LinkedIn, Facebook, and Gmail address book, and combine them with personal contacts kept in Outlook or Mac address, you will likely find that you can reach 1,000 people who know you. The potential for you to fit into a right-place right-time job with a personal connection is enormous, but only if you reach out to these people with an email and a link to your résumé.

You can repeat that outreach after eight to ten weeks if you still don't have the right kinds of opportunities in front of you. If your first outreach went out in July, your right-place, right-time opportunities may be appearing in September, and it will require another outreach in order for your contacts to see the connection. One friend who was looking for a job recently spent four months actively conducting the search without any concrete leads, then in one week he had three jobs to consider—none of which was open four months prior.

So your best and first opportunity is to flesh out of your broader world the immediate opportunities you could be considered for. Time is not on your side, so send a big, broad outreach, and without reservation. You can't know who your contacts know, so don't spend time eliminating people from your contact lists. The people who are working are voracious networkers. They reach out and understand that it works.

Closest Friend Outreach

This is more productive for you than it is for younger people, because you have more senior connections who know you well, and they collectively know thousands of people in influential positions. The basic close friend outreach (described in Chapter 9) is that you have five friends send twenty-five notes to people they know. For people over fifty, you should increase those numbers to ten friends and thirty-five to fifty connections. Ten people sending numerous notes to their influential contacts on your behalf would generate an enormous amount of targeted quality connections that will get serious consideration.

Reaching Protégés

There is another dimension that is not frequently addressed: The prior boss reaching out to former subordinates. My uncle used to tell me that I should be very good to the people who work for me, because someday I will probably work for one of them. We all want to think that we are the fast track and the idea of career hierarchy is fixed, but the fact is that no matter how exceptional we are, there are people who rocket up the ladder and eventually surpass us.

Very often, the fast climbers are voracious learners. They watch, listen, read, experiment, and glean from the best in an organization. They have an incredible ability to see the aspects that define excellence and see past those that define mediocrity. They are not just business geniuses, but often have mentors and talented people around them who play a role in their success.

Most rocket-risers are keenly aware about where their personal nuggets of wisdom came from. They appreciate the unique combination of leadership, functional skill, and political skill that got them to where they are. They realize that they have a blend of talents that define fast risers, but they also see enormous value in the strengths of people who may not have the same perfect blend of skills. They see people in terms of their strengths, not their weaknesses.

With this in mind, when a former boss reaches out to a prior subordinate, amazing things happen. First, as long as you were good to that person, you will be received with a huge, warm welcome. Why? Gratitude. Good bosses are hard to come by, and if you feel comfortable reaching out to someone you treated well in their early career, it suggests that the personal dynamic between the two of you was probably good. Since this person is successful, he/she will regard you as an integral part of this success.

That's a big cup of goodwill. He or she will also have a few other perspectives that you may not have. The first is one of learning. I have learned something from everyone I have worked for. People who rise up in companies almost always have some kind of unique talents. People who are successful recognize and learn from talented people. It's a natural symbiosis that is always present. But in the case of the subordinate, the fact that they learned from *you* means that they respect *you*. They are keenly aware of your strengths. They are grateful to you because of your strengths. Even if much time has gone by since you last worked together, and they are now far more proficient than you are in your own profession, their remembrance of you is a person of knowledge, expertise, and value.

So here you have a highly accomplished person who is grateful to you, who knows you, who respects you, and who would love nothing better than to help you in a meaningful way. Few things make somebody feel better than giving back to someone who gave so much to them. Don't let pride get in the way—the world is a big place and crazy things happen, but this is an asset that is too strong to overlook. It does require that the person has climbed the ladder at a good clip. You are looking for people with influence and connections at the levels that can help you.

Presenting Youthful Energy and Attitudes

Regardless of the company you are targeting, you should acknowledge that you are running head-on into an ageism bias. As an over-fifty person, I get to say this! I see it in Silicon Valley constantly, as the tech world is a very young business, and the people who win in tech are frequently so young that they have not yet been taught that what they are trying to do can't be done. Moreover, the concepts that young tech experts embrace are often foreign to older generations. Just to punctuate this point: Would an over-fifty person ever have conceived of the shared social networking elements on Facebook? The extraordinary popularity of Instagram?

So forgive me for addressing ageism in this book, as perhaps you think it is obvious, but there are elements to it that are important for you to know, because with this awareness, you can plan around it.

- Project youthful energy. If you think about the way young business people see things, you will appreciate that they have a bit of awe and excitement about the potential of cool, new ideas. They express great enthusiasm around these ideas. I mention this because part of the process of being in business for thirty years is that you've seen almost everything, and few things surprise you with a new view at opportunity. If you are headed into the right kind of company for an interview, you shouldn't find it too hard to find that passion, and by projecting enthusiasm, you help people see past your age.
- Be relevant. As humans, I like to say, "We all live in our own worlds." For the young person, that is a world of newness, change, what is cool, and whatever is the latest thing. In this changing world, knowing about the latest thing is just a part of being relevant. If you are interviewing for a job, and you fail to convey that you are aware of the definitional indicators of being in touch with a business or function, your interviewers will not see you as relevant. So you have your work cut out for you in approaching an industry. Before interviewing for the job, you need to set up meetings with at least three younger people in that industry and try to find out and feel the essence of newness and change in that space.
- Don't be Grandpa or Grandma. One of the interesting elements of perception is that it changes based on circumstance. Some wise people over fifty, when coming across a younger person in business (thirty-something) see them as a "headstrong teenager." Their natural social reaction is one of calm wisdom, gentle executive sharing, and guidance. It's a natural feeling for them, and they find it easy to fit into that role. However, while a person who is currently sitting in a senior executive job can project confidence with that approach, that same person when unemployed and interviewing comes across to the young person as Grandpa or Grandma. So, no matter how pompous or immature the person you are interviewing with is, focus on being the interviewee and not the wise advisor.

- Don't look like Mom or Dad. Personal appearance is a highly sensitive subject. On one hand, we are what we are. On the other hand, we all get used to ourselves and may fail to appreciate how the world sees us. When I look in the mirror, I see my twenty-seven-year-old self; it's only in pictures that I realize there is an extra several decades tacked on. With this in mind, you need to have your close friends beat you up on your haircut, your clothes, your shoes, and your watch. If you are dressed comfortably for you, there is a good chance that you look at lot like everybody's parent, and that makes it extremely hard for a hiring manager to see you in a role at their company. Here's a suggestion—when you set up the in-person meetings with people to gauge what the young view of an industry is, you need to ask them about the dress code and culture too. Steve Jobs always wore a black T-shirt and jeans. A permanently young look, and not for most companies, but imagine the impression Apple would have had of Jobs if he had worn a blue suit, white shirt, and red tie every day?

Key Takeaways:

- Follow all the steps in this book and leverage your strengths by adding extra emphasis to the personal network outreach, as your aim is to reach out to at least 500 people, and ideally many more, in this manner
- Double-up on the closest friend outreach by meeting with six to ten of your close friends and select twenty-to-fifty people that they can each send their endorsement intro to on your behalf. This should add another 200-300 or more excellent connections to your outreach
- Make sure to include prior protégés in your personal outreach and select a few of those for your in-person meetings
- Understand ageism and the approaches you can take to help the people you are interviewing see you as energetic, relevant, and a possible fit with the company

CHAPTER 20

Changing Professions

Most college kids change their majors at least once, and most adults strongly consider changing professions at some point in their work life. A career change is not for the faint of heart, but it can be the most rewarding and positive thing you can do. If you decide that the elements of an ideal job are just not possible within the profession you are in, it's time for you to look to the next stage of your working life.

Although changing jobs is very exciting, as it brings many new experiences, it also poses challenges, some of which may not be welcome. The challenges that may put some off changing careers are aptly described in *The Outliers* by Malcolm Gladwell, who states that, on average, it takes about 10,000 hours of practice to become proficient at something new. This concept has been studied and researched extensively, and many other authors are also citing 10,000 hours as the differentiating point for those who are getting compensated as an expert versus those who are in training.

So, when venturing into a new field, you should consider this: When are you going to get your 10,000 hours? Is it before you make the job change? That's hard, because 10,000 hours is five years of full-time work. But it is equally hard to get it on the job, because it almost certainly means that you will be making less money for the next three to five years.

Consider these two points:

1. What are the transferable skills you currently have that can be of value to a company you move to while you hold a position in your newly targeted field?
2. People who trust you the most are the ones most likely to help you find that bridge between where you are and where you want to go.

That intersection of the skills you have and your most trusted connections is likely to provide the path to your new life. Look to Chapter 10 again and think hard about how you are going to appear to others, and get advice from your closest friends on how to go about making the transition from your current career to the new field you are planning to target.

You will still want to go through all the steps we've previously described in this book. For career changing, it is important that you know what you want to do and can articulate which of your skills are going to translate well.

Winning Over the Hiring Manager

If somebody is going to consider taking a chance on you for this new field you are going into, if you are going to start at a higher salary and position than an entry level person, they are taking considerable risk. If you are coming in at entry level, you are facing a long road uphill unless you can demonstrate significant performance and growth quickly. The truth is that somebody will be willing to take a chance on you only if they can see the immediate value of your current skills and your potential to expand on them in the future. This, by the way, is far more desirable than starting over, so I'll focus on some things to think about to help make this happen.

As I discussed in Chapter 2, hiring managers are trying to identify individuals that represent the highest opportunity and the lowest level of risk. When changing careers, risk is mitigated if you get to that hiring manager through a connection, but is still real because you are not the ideal skill match. Hence, your challenge in the interview is to make this person believe, to the point that he or she is excited, that you are going to bring considerable value to this position.

Know the Industry

You are going to have a hard time getting the hiring manager to consider you if he or she feels that you don't understand the industry. To demonstrate that this is not the case, do your research, so that you are able to discuss, in the terms and the words used in the industry, the major strategic issues facing the key competitors, customers, and long-term industry challenges. This is the world of the hiring manager, and if you ask some insightful questions, it helps the hiring manager feel like you are in that same world. In short, you are demonstrating that you are truly interested in the space.

Demonstrated Intent

If you have worked in a different field your entire career, it helps if you have some evidence on your résumé and in your background that demonstrates your commitment to this new field. This can come many ways:

- College courses demonstrate a discipline and tenacity to truly learn and get a footing.
- You can also learn almost anything by studying information available on the Internet.
- Volunteer to work in the field.

- Find a hobby-oriented activity that is in the field or closely related to it.

The main point is that your time and your résumé should indicate that you are serious about working in this industry.

Key Takeaways:

- ➢ Think about how you are going to get your 10,000 hours of experience to develop a level of expertise that will be valued by employers
- ➢ Be able to articulate how your current skill-set translates to the new field, while you refine the new knowledge needed
- ➢ Your contacts are by far your best chance of connecting you with a hiring manager who will be open to considering you for your first job in this new industry
- ➢ Your challenge is to get the hiring manager to be excited about taking a risk on you. You can help make that happen through understanding the industry and demonstrating your knowledge and willingness to start afresh by learning and gaining practical experience related to the industry

CHAPTER 21

College Graduates

Recent college graduates can take advantage of unique opportunities despite mostly having no work experience. The first question they should answer before entering the job market is whether they have decided on a profession or not. If you are going into your senior year and neither your degree nor your desires are pointing you in a clear direction, study chapter 3 on the uncertain job seeker, this chapter, and set-up informational interviews in several fields of interest.

The Task of Selecting a Profession

Depending on how you draw the distinction, there are somewhere between 2,000 and 10,000 different kinds of jobs in the world. For discussion's sake, let's settle on 5,000. Part of the confusion of selecting a career is that most people are only aware of 50 to 200 different jobs and what they entail. Kids in college are typically aware of only half that number. Thus, it comes as no surprise that most would feel confused and unsure when faced with the prospect of selecting a profession.

Although there are many distinct jobs, they can be grouped into a smaller number of general categories, such as medicine, computer science, marketing, sales, finance, etc. So, from a high-level perspective, there are perhaps thirty or fifty different categories of work. The challenge is that each category has hundreds of different types of jobs within it. You could, for example, like the idea of mechanical engineering, but get into a job that you find horrible. Or, you could find a company, a team, and a project that is so terrific that you can't imagine anything better, even if your daily tasks are not exactly what you hoped to be doing. Still, with a limited view of the different types of jobs in engineering, most people, after the "horrible" experience, would quit the profession altogether.

A good friend of mine inherited his dad's insurance company, and he was mired in horrific customer, partner, and employee problems. He decided that not only was the insurance industry not for him, but after such an unpleasant experience, having any office job was inconceivable. He became a Park Ranger, which was a great career for him, but he'll never know if an executive-oriented position could have been a bigger opportunity that would also suit him well. If his first office job experience had been positive and productive, perhaps he would have chosen a different path.

The lesson here is to first recognize that, within categories of work, the jobs and experiences can be fundamentally different. You are setting out to identify a job that would offer you a potential to develop a career where you are:

- Deeply interested in the work, and
- Where you can add value to others

The typical description of the career for you is to do something you love, yet without the experience in a particular field, in a team dynamic, many college grads can't say in advance that there *is* something that they love as a profession. That's okay, you can start with something that you are deeply interested in. If it's something that you are only "sort of" interested in but you think that it would enable you to make a lot of money, you are heading into rough waters.

The other half of the coin is that you need to add value to others. That's a nice way of saying that you need to bring some combination of natural talent and developed skill to the job. In this case, I use the word "talent" to refer to the natural gifts you were born with. You might be naturally comfortable with people, or very responsible and detail-oriented, or you might be naturally compassionate. I use "skill" to refer to the knowledge and abilities you have developed and sharpened through your years of education and your hobbies. To make this even more thoughtful, also keep in mind your Triarchic Intelligence balance—analytic, creative, and intuitive. The decision you are trying to make when selecting your first job involves understanding your intelligences, skills and talents, and trying to identify that profession where you can be most engaged, most passionate, and most excited about producing spectacular results.

Internships

A good summer internship, particularly between your junior and senior year, is vitally important, as it will allow you to experience different types of work without having to commit to a full-time permanent job. The techniques in this book are *excellent* for your pursuit of an internship. Don't just rely on the company representatives that turn up at the university recruiting office. Get the best internship you can, and when you are there, try to meet as many other people in the company as you can, so that you can learn more about other jobs at that company.

Informational interviews

To make these important career decisions, one of the most helpful things you can do is to meet with working professionals, young and old, and seek to learn a bit about their professions and your fit. The rules related to making personal connections and meeting successful people still apply. You will find that, when approached by an enthusiastic youth, most senior people will be even more generous with their time and will try to help, even if your initial meeting is only informational. Follow Chapter 10 for the plan.

The difference with informational interviews is that you need to lead the discussion, as your goal is to find out as much as possible about the aspects of the work and the company you are curious about. You want to listen, to probe, and you want to paint a good picture of your talents and skills for the person you are meeting with. The better they understand you and your interests, the more they can help you. First, they can give you a very clear picture of how you might fit into their profession, and second, they will be able to suggest other professions for you to consider. Occasionally, you will be offered an introduction, so make sure to take that offer. When someone sees something in you, they will be keen to make an introduction, as their wisdom and experience might recognize a match that may not be obvious to you.

As with all meetings, you must follow up promptly with a thank-you note. This begins the important process of getting this person to be on your job search dream team. As discussed in Chapter 14, with conscientious follow-ups, you create involvement and a relationship where your contact becomes more interested in your success. As you identify the specific profession to target, you can go back to each of your contacts with a follow-up meeting requesting to talk about advice and connections that would help you to get the job you have decided to pursue. People want to help; they just need a little, tiny dose of respect and communication and they will open doors for you.

The Job Search

With your profession selected, you should start the actual job search, following somewhat modified strategies that were previously outlined. This will optimize the speed and ease of a job search for the college graduate.

Career center

Your school's career center is a good starting point when it comes to résumé preparation and on-campus interviews. Make sure that you understand all the different opportunities that your career center provides.

Job-posting sites

Although I advise working professionals to avoid responding to job postings as a college grad, you should spend some time reviewing postings and applying to the ones that are most compelling. Companies need new people every year, and although you should still focus on personal connections, you should pursue this avenue too, as many people get jobs through job postings. Your career center will have the best sources in your area, but as of this writing, Monster.com, Craigslist.com, indeed.com, and others should have options.

Résumé -posting sites

Most of the same sites also accept résumé postings, which you should do, as noted in Chapter 6.

Recruiting firms

Most of the recruiting firms are focused on people with substantial work experience, but a few firms do handle recent grads. You will want these firms to have your résumé, and some of the firms may want you to come in for an interview.

Personal network outreach

Follow the steps outlined in Chapter 8 exactly—reach up and out to people in the workforce through family, family friends, friends' parents, ex-coaches, etc. This implies getting the emails or phone numbers of people that you don't have. Start early in your senior year to gather this contact information. Create your own personal contact list in Outlook or your Mac address. Kids use Facebook and their phone, but working professionals keep a thorough contact list, so as you prepare to enter the workplace, you should slowly make this transition.

You also have a big opportunity to connect with the people one class ahead of yours. Develop relationships with seniors when you are a junior, which you can do when attending the same classes. Make sure that some of the seniors know you for the quality of your work. Reach out to the recently hired graduates once or twice in the fall of your senior year to ask for career advice, and ask for referrals and introductions in late winter.

New hires that are performing well are typically asked by the company to refer more good people, as it is assumed that good people know good people. Make sure that you know many good people who are older than you are. If you manage to develop a friendship, recent grads will have some level of emotional attachment to you and will thus work hard to think of you as the sum total of all your strengths. Otherwise, they will not have much incentive to help you, as they will not know you well and will perceive you as a combination of some strengths, some weaknesses, and a lot of risk . . . .

In-person meetings

The process of in-person meetings may be a little harder while you are in college, as the people in your broader social network may be too far away to meet with. Plan this process well in advance, so that if your university is in one city, your target job is in another city, and your connections are largely in your hometown, you find the time and place to organize and attend the in-person meetings. That means that you have to make sure to complete all the local meetings while school is in session. Carefully set up the personal connection meetings when you are at home for summer, fall, or during the winter break. And through both the local and "back home" personal connections, get introductions to people in your target job city so that you can also schedule to spend one week in that city before mid-winter.

Please remember that your easiest job search and your best shot at an ideal job will always come through this avenue. Don't subordinate these steps to other elements of your job search.

Alumni power

Some schools do a better job than others at helping kids reach out to alumni for help in getting started after graduating. But no matter how well your school helps with this, alumni outreach is an amazingly effective option that few understand or take advantage of. The massive scale of your college alumni is hard to comprehend. Let's say that 3,000 people graduate every year from your university and, on average, each will work for thirty-five years; that means that there are over 100,000 people working today who you can reach out to.

The influence that these alumni represent is mind-boggling. Here's why. First, the alumni status is your personal connection. It is an affiliation that, for whatever reason, acts as if there is a prior personal connection in that people you reach out to will want to help you, and they will be flattered that you asked. Part of the psychology of this is that most people think of their college years as the best time of their life. Exuberant youth, great friends, great hopes, and great fears are things everybody remembers fondly. By reaching out to these people, you walk in the door with the youthful energy that they hold onto so dearly in their memories. It's just fun for them to meet with you. If you are articulate and respectful, they will likely want to help.

The other reason is that because there are so many alumni, you can find many alumni working in every one of those 5,000 different jobs. Want to know more about a certain profession? Call an alumnus. Want to know more about available jobs at the most successful companies in America? Call an alumnus. You have a cornucopia of opportunities.

And what is most amazing: most alumni ARE NEVER ASKED. In my own informal checks with some of the most accomplished people I know—top investment bankers, fortune 500 CEOs, top technology industry executives—not one has been asked by a new college graduate for a meeting to discuss career options. It does happen, of course, but for some reason this superhighway to success is missed.

Caution: The LinkedIn mistake. I recommend that you do not try to reach Alumni on LinkedIn, as this is becoming too easy and is often seen as annoying. People working at the marquis companies like Google are pestered too often from new grads through link requests, and they become numb to the prospect of helping others. It is much better to get the email addresses of the alumni you would like to meet, and send them a note, or call, to ask for a meeting.

Half of the college grads in America have not found work, and yet how many of them have approached any of their 50,000 to 300,000 alumni?

The Internet offers numerous ways to find people and professions. Start by typing your profession and university into LinkedIn. Try the university alumni registry. The Internet and connections will make it possible for you to find people, and somewhere between one-third and one-half of the people you ask will meet with you. So find twenty, ask them all, and see what happens.

Follow the guidelines in Chapters 10 through 14, as you want these people to be on your job search dream team, and you want to establish a lifetime connection with them.

The alumni connection response will likely be good, but because they do not have that direct personal relationship with you, you have to earn their trust in order to get a referral. Ask for a meeting on career advice, and try to get the in-person meeting, if at all possible. They need to meet you, look you in the eye, see your earnestness, your humbleness, your deference, your confidence, and your willingness to work hard. They need to hear you ask interesting questions. They need to understand more about what you can do, what your personal strengths are, and how you think. To help build this spirit of goodwill, invite them to meet with you on campus—this brings them out of their skeptical world and into the world of their alma mater–youth energy, and possibilities.

An alumnus needs to correlate all these factors about you with the things they know and the people they know. As long as you have a fairly clear direction of where you want to go, they can work on a solution and will soon be offering you connections and ideas for job sourcing. If you are not clear, then you are fishing or exploring, and if you are exploring, they are off the hook—all pressure is off them, and they can just pontificate about all the things that you could/should do.

If you strike even a small amount of chemistry with a person you establish contact with or ideally meet, you have a good chance of getting a connection. If chemistry is lacking, you will not get anything meaningful. If offered an introduction, it is a HUGE olive branch offer—this person is willing to give you a gift, solely out of the generosity of his or her heart. That is the beginning of a relationship. With the right thank-you note (remember to send an email within the first twenty-four hours), and the right follow-up correspondence (both to the person that has introduced you and the people you have met through them), and a few general status updates, you have now brought this person into your Job Search Dream Team, and he or she will work on your behalf with more connections.

Key Takeaways:

- Of some 5,000 different professions, people are only aware of 50-100 different careers. Exploration and open-mindedness are essential when unsure of which career path you wish to follow. Before selecting a profession, you should have informational interviews with at least fifteen people working in and around the different professions that you are considering
- For job finding, follow the steps in the book, and take advantage of the career center services and on-campus interviewing
- You should apply extra effort and planning to build-out your personal connections including people in the class ahead of yours, as well as people in your hometown
- Alumni are a particularly good way to generate connections and job opportunities, yet very few college kids reach out to this group of people who have a soft spot in their hearts for graduates from their alma mater

CHAPTER 22

Veterans

Veterans should follow the strategies defined in this book, but with one huge addition: as their status commands immediate and well deserved respect, this creates an advantage, as a veteran can ask for a meeting with anybody who is an American citizen. While not all people will agree to meet, if the request is executed well, it will bring many positive responses. You have the ability to get a meeting with most professionals, regardless of their level, as most people feel a sense of obligation to help someone who was willing to risk their life for their country. This represents a terrific and limitless opportunity.

Inside the Mind of the Successful Working Vet

Veterans are a proud bunch. They hold on to their experience in the service with reverence and respect. Veterans who have been successful in business seem to look at their time in the service as an essential element of their success. Given that tenacity is the single most-cited factor for success, and productivity requires discipline, the link between success and the service is obvious.

If the typical successful person wants to help and is flattered when you ask, the successful vet is twice as anxious to help and twice as flattered. One of the most consistent aspects about vets is the bond they share among each other, particularly in the same branch of service. A request for advice from a fellow marine, for example, is just too easy to grant and too important to turn down. Add to this the dynamic that vets also have a naturally strong desire to help their country and you will see that the chance of being turned down is rather small. America has had a voluntary military for a long time; most working vets today volunteered, with the exception of some Vietnam vets. The ability to serve your country, help the economy, and do something positive for a fellow vet all adds up to somebody you should reach out to.

Inside the Mind of the Non-Vet

When it comes to veterans, the mindset of most people, including hiring managers that have not served in the armed forces, is one of obligation and respect. Deep down, people who have not served know that they owe a debt to the people who did. They know that the debt is huge, ominous. The idea of putting oneself into a war zone and not being able to just run away is more of a commitment than most people can comprehend.

This sense of debt is what I call "Freedom Rider." Okay, this does not have a very positive connotation, but let's put aside pleasantries and political correctness. People who enjoy the benefits of liberty in America but have not served to protect it are riding on the backs of those who have served. Freedom is not free, as the bumper sticker says. I too am a Freedom Rider, and I am keenly aware of it.

Vets, by approaching people with humility and respect, by sharing how you admire their success and would appreciate a meeting to talk about career options, you will ensure that your note is received in an enormously positive spirit. You elicit in those you contact the best of the desires to help a vet, and you open their minds as to how. Personalize your initial communication by having a picture of you in your uniform with some buddies to share. It's a heart-felt reaction for any person to see a vet in uniform in service who is asking for career advice.

All vets are given credit for being disciplined, responsible, reliable, and tenacious. These are rare and valued qualities in today's world. Be very confident in knowing that you have your own combination of the three intelligences, and your own development of skills and talents, which can bring tremendous value to the right company.

I suggest that your in-person meeting requests start with your direct and indirect personal connections, and then include several influential people you don't know but are in the field you want to work in. Do your research online to identify which companies and which people in those companies would be good to target. Use veteran directories to identify vets who are in business. Make sure to get two or three meetings per day. Your experience from these meetings will be energizing, motivating, and exciting. Every day something positive will happen that will increase your confidence and strengthen your resolve to pursue your chosen career.

When you do meet with somebody who you do not have a personal connection with, remember that you still have to earn their trust to get a recommendation. This may not happen as often as you like, but remember that they have given you the gift of time, and with that time, they will give you advice, some of which will be excellent. Be keenly aware of the details in Chapter 11 regarding the qualities of a person who gets referrals. If you are articulate, respectful, and clear about your strengths and your target job, ideas will start coming to the person you are meeting with. As this contact becomes more comfortable with you, it becomes easier for him or her to take the risk of introducing you to somebody else.

From the perspective of vets who may have a physical impairment or PTS, consider this: It is much easier to deal with the hard parts of life when you have a daily positive experience that provides personal validation, friendship, hope and opportunity. Humans thrive on hope and opportunity. It is what we are best at. Not blind hope. Not hope for an easy life, but hope that you will be given the opportunity to do spectacular things.

The people you meet with will also help you to appreciate benefits and drawbacks of different types of jobs, and will draw connections between your unique skills, your desires, and the types of careers that might be best for you. As you learn more about different careers, a wonderful symbiosis occurs. The jobs that would enable you to truly excel start to be presented from unexpected places. If you meet with several people on a daily basis, you have a good chance of surfacing more than one opportunity, and with several jobs to interview for, you'll start to see the clarity of why you can and will find your ideal job.

And when you are in your ideal job, you will wake up excited to go to work and immerse yourself in the essence of problem solving at work. You will find that the satisfaction of being appreciated, productive, and part of a team is a wonderful way to focus your mind and your energy on your new path. The urgency of the challenge of the job creates an undercurrent of positive stress that forces the mind to focus, and when you are truly focused on creating and producing excellent results, you are on your way.

Key Takeaways:

- More than any group of people in America, veterans have the ability to reach out to any successful person and be well received
- Successful vets (not capitalized before) in your same branch of service abound, and they want to help you
- Be confident in your unique value to companies through your combination of personal intelligences, skills and talents, together with the valued qualities of discipline and tenacity that you acquired in the service
- Follow all the outreach and career site posting elements in the book, focusing primarily on asking for meetings with senior and influential people

SECTION V

Action Time

Knowledge is power, but only if you use it

CHAPTER 23

Beware of Digital Diversion

The evolution of technology in the last thirty years has changed the fundamental ways we connect with people. Below, I have broken it down into three categories of technology that have changed the way we live our daily lives and have affected the way humans have lived for thousands of years. We were not shaped and formed this way, and in a very real way each of these categories replaces relationship building:

- Addictive Diversion: Video games, TV shows, and digital entertainment are all designed to be enjoyed alone (or at least not looking at each other eye to eye)
- Voyeurs in other people's lives: Reality shows represent billions of hours of time people spend watching other people instead of engaging with other people. YouTube also fits in this category
- Digital connecting: Social networking (Facebook, LinkedIn), texting, IM, Pinterest, Twitter have probably been envisaged to allow long lost friends to connect and to link people from different parts of the world, but have fast replaced communications even amongst (among before) people that could be easily reached in person

Social Networking Is a Misnomer

The massive growth of social networking is a fascinating sociological change, as both personal information shared through Facebook and professional information posted on LinkedIn have increased the 'visibility' of every person using these services. But the category name of "social networking" is rather odd. Social refers to people interacting on a personal basis, which I would argue is not sharing photos and stories of your day with hundreds of people at once. Nor is it messaging through a proprietary interface like Facebook. Networking is the process of meeting with people and being introduced to new people through others. These sites establish a digital link, and people somehow seek other digital links, but there isn't a lot of networking going on. I refer to this category of sites as:

"Non-social digital linking"

In the non-social digital linking world, you can post all kinds of details about your life, you can see all sorts of things about other people's lives, and nothing beats this medium for immediacy and awareness. These sites become your personal website available for people to peruse, sharing a growing scrapbook of your life. To a great degree, it's fun and it's quite informative for people to see who you are.

But what an interesting phenomenon: Who has time to review the living and breathing scrapbooks of life of hundreds of other people? Many people, evidently; although average user time on Facebook is declining, people still spend many hours exchanging messages, pictures and ideas with others.

Although there is the opportunity for one-on-one communication through these sites, building a meaningful relationship by doing so is unlikely. More typically, the connection on these sites locks in whatever the depth of a relationship was at the point of connecting. This is important, because the process of having a broad and trusted network of friends requires the building and strengthening of relationships, which can only happen in person.

At the other extreme is how many people link to each other on the non-social digital linking sites with little or no personal connection. This expands the number of people connected, which carries a status, but it means that hundreds of links are established among people who have not met and most likely have no intention to do so. Teenagers do this so much that there is a game they play: One person gets on a friend's Facebook page, randomly selects a person in that friend list, and then asks the owner of the friend list if they know who it is! I have many people on my own LinkedIn that I can't identify, and some on Facebook. These sites have developed what I call *"an exponential capability to connect you with people you do not care about."*

I'll explain how this exponential growth translates to a reduction in the fundamentals of relationship building. Think of relationships as having five levels of depth:

1. Closest friends
2. Friends—people you see regularly and occasionally socialize with
3. Good acquaintances—people you are familiar with, find interesting, but do not socialize with
4. Acquaintances—people you have met a few times, you know their names, you cross paths occasionally
5. Somebody you once met, or might have once met, but don't remember

In a heavily active digital linking world, the first two levels are mostly unaffected. However, the third and fourth levels of social circles are withering, and the fifth level is exploding.

Levels Three and Four

In levels three and four, the process of discovering new people with similar interests on a relationship level is lessened, as that group that you would normally evolve into a relationship is now "locked in" as a connection on Facebook or LinkedIn. Instead of making an effort to meet for lunch or a drink, people confirm that a person is in their social network and are satiated. In a world before social networking, people spent more time gathering, meeting, looking eye to eye, and being intrigued by a new person. Mutual interest would lead to a lunch, a sport, etc.

In the non-social digital linking world, however, people spend time sitting on the computer, posting their daily actions, and reading about other people's actions. Instead of connecting in person with others, they read about somebody's tuna sandwich and another person's cat. The odd thing is this: Seeing this person's name and their personal life unfold on a regular basis replaces the age-old dynamic of suggesting that they connect in person. These foggy digital acquaintances rarely get a chance to evolve into friendships. These are the elements that break down community—the community that naturally builds relationships that foster trust and builds multi-tiered connections that create opportunity.

Level Five

Level five connections are the people who you've met once (maybe), and this has always represented the largest group. The simple pathways of life bring us across many people, and some people are in this outer circle because they represent some kind of relevance to us. They may be a friend of a friend or somebody you see occasionally in the neighborhood. In a world before social networking, this was always a group of people that were mostly inconsequential in your world.

With social networking sites, the result of this ease of connecting is that your world becomes cluttered with hundreds of people who are inconsequential to you. Hence, the reason I like to say that social networking has given us the exponential ability to connect with people we don't care about.

This is a fascinating trade-off. We are essentially filling up our time and attention with people who are inconsequential, and since we are spending so much time on the computer and not in front of people, we are spending far less time with new and different people in person. We are spending far less time building relationships.

There Are Only Twenty-four Hours in a Day

With this social disconnection as a framework, when we add up all the time spent in the three categories of digital diversion the only possible result is the steady decline in the number of meaningful relationships. The addictive diversion of gaming is by itself a significant shift in the way teenage boys allocate time in their days. You can't spend six hours a day gaming and also spend three or four hours a day with friends playing sports. Or better yet, in a pre-digital world you had to spend three to four hours a day with friends trying to think of creative things to do. Joint problem solving, aligning of interests and people, shared adventure . . . mostly lost, yet excellent for relationship building.

The voyeuristic and voluminous nature of TV today is another element that has carved out a large section of a person's life and isolated them from others. Reality shows tell stories of wacky people in conflict-generating circumstances that we find mesmerizing. Isn't that interesting? The vast majority of America prefers to watch other people lead interesting lives rather than trying to make their lives more interesting and fulfilling. Why? It's easy, available, and the show producers have become experts at filling the shows with exciting tension.

So, here is our world, where we have girls spending hours on Facebook, texting and IMing, boys gaming in most of their free time, and the adults buried in endless TV. There aren't enough hours left in the day for people to get together to find new friends, meet new people, and build new relationships. The events that used to bring people together are becoming fewer and farther between.

Digital Diversion Makes Success Easier

In a world of increasing relationship disconnection, it is *amazingly easy to succeed.* Why? Because so few people truly understand that you get jobs through people, not computers, and the way you get jobs through people is by establishing meaningful relationships with them. When only a few people actually understand this, you have a wide-open field of people to ask for help, with very few people being "worn out" from too many impersonal requests.

A relationship based on trust does not have to require a lifetime of commitment. In fact, part of the acceleration of our lives through technology means that people tend to grasp the time they do have with people and focus deeply to maximize their use of that time. Eye-to-eye meetings with good intentions and mutual interests are a quick way to develop a bit of a desire to connect in a positive way.

Now think about the relationship-building possibilities using all those somewhat unknown people in your LinkedIn and Facebook. Within your current connections, there are some people whom you don't know very well, yet they may be people you would get along with and who could be professionally beneficial to you. Some people "meet" first on Facebook and then in person. So your digital linking can be used to mine for a potential person of integrity, trust and success, as you have a fair amount of public information to make a judgment call about who to meet.

As you come to appreciate that digital diversion is a problem and hinders your personal competitive advantage in the job market, you will begin to fall back on the core elements of being human. These are the ingredients of creating the trust that makes people help others.

- Humans look into each other's eyes
- Humans give energy
- Humans share experiences
- Humans help each other
- Humans stimulate discourse
- Humans share smiles
- Humans hear the emotion in your voice
- Humans support
- Humans teach
- Humans stand up for friends
- Humans reinforce your best potential
- Humans believe in you enough to get you the job

As the digital diversion has exploded, and non-social digital linking has grown exponentially in its efficiency, your time and energy are overwhelmed with irrelevant connections that take you away from the meaningful relationships.

Key Takeaways:

- ➢ Normal life today is structurally designed to minimize relationship building
- ➢ Understanding the simple value of an in-person meeting gives you an advantage versus others in getting people to refer you and help you find a job
- ➢ Facebook and LinkedIn provide an opportunity for identifying people who can help your career, and if you are connected on one of these sites, rather than sending endless messages, ask for an in-person meeting

CHAPTER 24

The Greatest Risk

Our world is filled with employment discontent, as most of us are unhappy at work and too many are out of work. While it is obvious why the unemployed would not be content with their status, it is fascinating and rather surprising that, according to a recent Right Management survey, 86% of all employed people plan to get a new job "next year."

Clearly, these people are not in their ideal jobs. Everybody has a reason for dissatisfaction—many people feel underemployed as they took whatever job they could in tough times. Others stay in jobs because they need the paycheck, and the upside of a regular check is better than the downside of looking for another job–or worse, being without a job. Others are on the path they set for themselves twenty years ago and they feel that they no longer have any options. Nevertheless, the one way to describe all of the unhappily employed is that they have settled.

This is a fascinating perspective. The vast majority of people settle for something less than they want. One explanation is simply that the human species is the most adaptive species on the planet—people adapt to snow, deserts, altitude, and just about everything else Mother Nature can throw our way. So while it may be seen as harsh to describe this "adaptation" as settling, the fact is that people are not in jobs they are excited to be in.

Now think about this from the angle of productivity. Years of research and empirical evidence indicate that people who are not happy and energized in their jobs are not as productive as those who are. The element of passion and the energy of excitement stimulate the most creative elements within us all, and the positive energy is infectious for those around us. A team of passionate and excited people can produce truly spectacular results, but a team of people who feel trapped in something that is not quite right has a hard time being productive.

I have been in both scenarios in my career. When I have been in jobs where the blend of opportunity and the right team were in place, the energy level was high, the possibilities seemed endless, and my satisfaction was evident in the results I produced. On the other hand, the jobs where I couldn't find the opportunity, or the fit with my skills was just not good, made it very hard for me to find a level of productivity that would be above average. Okay, the reality is that I had a hard time finding even acceptable productivity. When work feels like work, and it takes tremendous mental energy to force yourself to stay connected, it is quite hard to produce at a high level.

From the perspective of your career, this is worth a long and deep reflection. Why are you staying in that job? What is it that you have told yourself to make it feel like the best decision? I will challenge you to consider this:

> *The riskiest thing you can do is to stay in a job you are not excited to be in. Your work will not be up to your potential, your management will not perceive you in the best light, you will not be identified as the first in line for a promotion, you will not be recommended as often by your peers, and you will not be sought after by recruiters.*

People end up in dead-end jobs because they settle early for work that is not their ideal job. Dead-end jobs have a way of turning into dead-end careers.

But Wait, It Gets Worse

The emotional and mental strain of staying in the dead-end work environment is exhausting, and it spills over into your personal life. You have less energy for all the trials and tribulations that life brings us. Your relationship with your spouse is strained, or your energy to find that future spouse is tapped. Your optimism about all things is blunted. And if you have kids, all the patience that is required every minute you are around them seems hard to bring forward.

So I will ask again: What have you told yourself that makes you think this is a good choice? It is one of the craziest, literally craziest, parts of being human. We desperately want recognition, we have a strong desire to contribute, we want to help others, to create and to succeed, and yet the great vast majority of people settle.

The rational answer to the "why" is Fear, Uncertainty and Doubt:

- Fear that you may get caught looking for a new job and get fired
- Uncertainty that you don't know exactly what to do to be considered for a certain job
- Doubt that even if you do go on the journey to find your ideal job, you won't find it

I find that most people have not seen their work-life as the pursuit of the ideal job—the pursuit of that place where excitement and immersion bring forward their greatest work. A place where they surprise themselves with the kinds of things they can produce. Isn't it time that you defined this for yourself?

I would argue that even if finding a new job was the most painful thing to do, you should run, not walk, to the start-line of your new job search.

But with the clarity that settling is the riskiest thing you can do, and with the plan spelled out in this book that shows you how finding your ideal job can be easy, energizing, and mind-expanding, perhaps it is time for you to chart your course. Don't cheat yourself out of your future, your potential and your dreams.

With this in mind, imagine how your world would change if you shed the fear, the uncertainty and the doubt. You would confidently set yourself on a course to find your ideal job, and when you found it, you would hold on to it and do all you could to succeed. Imagine how your whole world would change if you did this.

This new way of thinking will shift you from adapting and settling to being in active control of your life and your career happiness. You will pour yourself into your work, create things you never knew you could, and discover an entirely new level of job satisfaction. The more time you spend doing what you love, the more expertise you develop and, with that, you will soon be in high demand. The more you are in demand, the easier it is to feel in complete control of your life.

If and when your ideal job changed because of a new boss, a different vision, or any number of factors, you would be prepared with connections and options so the feeling of impending doom would not appear.

You would start to see every job change as an opportunity to find a fantastic, new, personal adventure, and that adventure would embrace you.

With this final thought, I wish for you the courage and optimism to set your life path as an ongoing search to be in, and find, your ideal job. I would say good luck, but the theme here is to take luck out of the process, so instead, I will say "looking forward to you creating spectacular things."

Key Takeaways:

- The vast majority of people are unhappy with their work
- It is almost impossible to produce your best work if you are unhappy, hence settling is the riskiest thing you can do for your career
- With the understanding that following the plan in this book would make finding your ideal job easy, is there any reason to stay?
- When you decide for yourself to never settle, you see the world differently, as you pursue your ideal job

CHAPTER 25

The "Easy" Plan Summarized

- First, read the paragraph below out loud today and every day until you have your job. It is important for you to fully absorb these concepts for the process to feel easy and energizing:

  I have decided to never settle for a job that I am not excited about, and not stay in a job out of fear of what might come next. Since no one can be successful alone, I have promised myself to create and follow a plan to arrange meetings with influential personal connections. And although it makes me feel vulnerable, I remind myself that a request for advice is seen by others as confidence and strength. So I commit to ask for advice about career perspectives, résumé feedback, and job leads. I boldly reach up to the most powerful people who know me or know of me, grounded in the truth that successful people want to help and they are flattered when I ask. I take a deep breath and remind myself of this again: they are flattered when I ask. I recall how good I feel following these meetings, and their smiles convince me that they felt the same. I know that this is the essential social fabric of humanity, and I only need to offer a formal thank you in exchange - the gesture with the benefit of building enduring relationships and not eroding them. I move forward everyday with relentless tenacity because I know that as long as I am aware of my ignorance, and at the same time confident in my ability to learn, I will succeed.

- Second, Get Set: The process of getting set should be no more than one week, by working everyday on your résumé and refining your definition of your target job. Engage a professional résumé writing service for your fastest result.
- Third, Get in the Game:
    - Day one should be spent getting in the game by accessing the right career sites, sending your data to the right recruiting firms, and sending an outreach note to hundreds of your contacts
    - Day two through five should be used for meetings with your closest friends, where you work with them to send an intro/endorsement letter of you to twenty-five or more of their connections with a résumé link attached
- Fourth, Get Connected: Day six-onward should be organized so that you set up and attend meetings with senior and influential people in your extended personal network, to seek advice and introductions. Take Control: Every day you should send thank-you notes, track referrals, ask for more meetings, and review your overall plan, as outlined in this book.
- *Do not spend time browsing web sites and applying for job postings. That's a downward spiral with little positive returns.*

Now is the time for you to get on the Fast Track to Your Ideal Job!

People who are currently unemployed do not have time on their side. The unfortunate reality is that the longer you are out of work, the more people wonder if there is some reason that you are not getting the job you want. If you are unhappily employed, time has a relentless pace. It is not forgiving, and it is not patient.

Your decision to get started involves a significant shift away from your prior experience and perspectives. The old approach to job finding tears down a person's inner confidence. You do a lot of work, presenting yourself to hundreds of people for their approval and interest, and almost nobody comes back to you. You spend time on the computer endlessly writing cover letters and filling out job applications with very little response. The occasional interview is hard to get excited about because the job seems beneath you. You dread waking up in the morning, as the "sting" of the harsh reality that you need a job hits hard. You dread getting started with your "full-time job" of job hunting, because the tasks are so obscure, so voluminous, and so tedious.

As time passes, you second-guess yourself every day: Am I spending my time effectively? Should I be connecting with recruiters? You have the constant pressure of human vulnerability: What if I don't get another job? Why is this so hard? At a time when you need energy the most, these things sap your personal energy and with it your optimism.

With the techniques in this book, you will find that the job search process becomes one of the most energizing times of your life. You spend almost no time on the computer, and you only fill out job applications where you have an inside connection. You spend your time, day in and day out, meeting with people who know you or give you instant credibility as referrals from mutual friends. When you meet with people, the magic of the best of humanity comes to play—infectious enthusiasm.

Your contacts and friends validate you, reminding you that you are a successful, capable person. They remind you that change is opportunity, and with opportunity, there is potential. You laugh and share stories about how purely insane the world of work is and how unpredictable people can be. You brainstorm about new ideas for work or connections. They tell you about the people they know whom you should meet. It is one of the most energizing things we can do as humans.

From the moment you make the decision to look for another job, the clock starts ticking. Every day, you need to spend your time on the activities that can make the most difference.

And with that, you are on your way to a great future.

Appendix

A: The Blue Chip Solutions

Full disclosure: as I mentioned in the preface of this book, I have created a website that automates many of the strategies in the book. The website is not necessary to get the benefits and strategies outlined in the preceding chapters, but it can save time and is designed to make the entire process easy. As of the time of this writing, much of the value of Blue Chip sites is available for no charge, so there is little risk in exploring it.

The initial Blue Chip site is BlueChipExec.com, and we plan to expand the availability of Blue Chip services to different segments:

- BlueChipExec.com, for all white collar and professional workers
- BlueChipGrad.com, for college students in preparation of their first job
- BlueChipVet.com, for military veterans
- BlueChipJobs.com, for people working outside of office environments
- BlueChipExpert.com, for freelancers and consultants

These solutions empower you to accomplish more with your job search in one week than most people do in months. And you will not only do the work, but the right kind of work, as you will focus on being noticed and getting action.

Once you have your résumé and your job objectives sorted out, you are ready to get started.

As articulated in the book, the Blue Chip Solution will help you "Get in the Game," effectively launching your job search with such coverage and intensity that you may just be busy reacting to the opportunities that come your way. The process of "Getting in the Game" with Blue Chip Exec takes about forty-five minutes and includes:

- Matching your profile and background to the career sites suited for you, then getting your information on to those sites.
- Matching your profile and background to the recruiting firms that conduct searches for jobs like the one you are looking for, and getting your information to those rezcruiters. The range is between three and 600 recruiter matches, and the average is about 100. The more senior you are in business, the more recruiters you will be matched with, as most of the recruiting firms specialize in senior positions.
- Enabling you to send a personalized outreach to your personal and professional networks, automatically uploading and organizing your contacts, providing a pre-written email template that you can customize, and including a link to your résumé. This, the most powerful of the Get-in-the-Game steps, should go out to hundreds of people you know.

After your first day of "getting in the game," Blue Chip makes it easy for you to get connected with just fifteen minutes of work per day. It provides a professional relationship management feature, called the Career Relationship Manager, that will assist you in asking for meetings and tracking the scheduled meetings, and will also allow you to follow up with thank-you notes, keep a record of the source of referrals, and follow-on actions with referrals.

Lastly, Blue Chip provides the project management and reminder support to make getting results easy. You are provided with daily coaching that points you toward the most effective next step you should take for your search. You also get a dashboard that presents the status of your overall job search, with suggestions on the most urgent next steps and links to make those steps easy.

And it gets better! Once you are in a new position, Blue Chip makes it easy to wrap up your search that helps improve your relationships and keeps you in view of the top recruiting firms. They update all the recruiters with your current information, showing you as an employed person at your new company. You never know when the right *next* job will be looking for you. Blue Chip then makes it easy to notify and thank all your contacts and the people who helped you with your job search.

This puts you in an excellent position to keep up with the networking and tracking of important relationships for the Career Relationship Manager. Now that you have experienced the power of relationship-building networking, you will be excited to keep up your good practices, and the Blue Chip Exec company sites can make that easy.

B: One Page Refreshers

(SAMPLE REVERSE CHRONOLOGICAL RESUME) *This is the standard option for most people. It is best for people with jobs that are in different categories and with different/increasing levels of responsibility.*

Jane Doe
Jane.Doe@dmail.com

238 Ashbury Street
Richmond, VA 23223
804-300-5000

SUMMARY

In this section list a high level summary about who you are. Include a top level description of your overall level, your areas of specialization, your best strengths, and a message about how you deliver results. This section is typically two or three lines for new grads, or 5-6 lines for more senior execs. e.g. Senior Marketing Research executive with extensive experience in leading large teams in both industrial and consumer products. Part of senior leadership team contributing to the creation of company strategic plans, identification of new business opportunities, and streamlining processes. Significant results in quantifying areas of opportunity in customer relations, product improvement, technical support, as well as numerous one-off studies. Specific strengths include detail orientation, analytic skills, complex study design and execution, and perspectives for long term strategic impact.

EXPERIENCE (list in reverse chronology)

Magnifico Inc. Houston, TX
Vice President, Marketing Research, (August 2009 to present)
• Describe the general business that the company is in. One line. e.g. Recruited to lead marketing research for this $11Billion company in the industrial valve category.
• Describe your areas of responsibility – two-three lines, be specific. E.g. Responsible for leading a team of 9 with a budget of $12.4M, in the creation and execution of marketing research across 6 product lines and 4 continents.
• Describe significant results, with data for each result. Two to four lines. e.g. Successfully contributed to the identification of three new product group categories, and helped form the customer value propositions for 4 new geographies. Completed 5 global surveys with key decision makers which has contributed to 6 customer service processes and manufacturing improvements in 4 plants.

Tribulator Co. Chicago, IL
Senior Direct, Marketing Research, (January 2006 to August 2009)
• Describe the general business that the company is in. This is meant to help the reader get some perspective about your work, there are thousands of companies and industries, so don't assume anybody knows your company
• Describe your areas of responsibility – If promoted to this position, list it. this is meant to help the reader understand what you have been entrusted with, and frame the scope of the results you should be able to achieve within your areas of responsibility. Beware of using acronyms, essentially, there should be zero three letter acronyms on your resume.
• Describe significant results, with data for each result. This is your chance to showcase your performance

Director, Marketing Research, (July 2004 to December 2005)
• Describe your areas of responsibility – When listing multiple positions within the same company, you do not need to list the description of the company's business, unless this role is a different division than the previous one listed.
• Describe significant results, with data for each result. This should be written in a way that shows such good results that it warrants the promotion or new role you had within the same company

Add all companies, or limit detail to past 20 years. If you have more than 20 years experience, just list the first companies and titles you had without taking too much room for accomplishments.

EDUCATION

MIT, Master of Science in Statistics Boston, May 1998
University of Norfolkshire, Bachelor of Science in Mathematics Becketts Bay, Maine, May 1995

(SAMPLE FUNCTIONAL RESUME-EXPERIENCED INDIVIDUAL) *This is a good option if the responsibilities, skills and results have been similar for many years of work in several different jobs. It is done typically to avoid having each company description sound like the one before it, none of which giving much depth. Consequently, the skill areas in this resume need to paint an excellent picture of capabilities and experience. Answer the question, what can this person do for me?*

JOHN Q. WORKER
14445 Ridge View
Laguna Beach, California 92812
(714) 555-1212
John.q.worker@ggmail.com

SUMMARY

In this section list a high level summary about who you are. Include a top level description of your overall level, your areas of specialization, your best strengths, and a message about how you deliver results. This section is typically two or three lines for new grads, or 5-6 lines for more senior execs.

SKILLS

Skill X: In this area describe a functional skill you possess. Give perspective about how many years you have been working with this skill, give dimension on how far along you are relative to the industry standards, share whether you teach this skill to others, whether you lead a team of others about this skill. List high level results with the skill.

Skill Y: Each skill should have a similar cadence to the description of the skill, the examples and the results

Skill Z:
5 or 6 major skills

EXPERIENCE

>> List in reverse chronology

Horatio Co. Wilkersonville, WY
Title, (August 2009 to present)
• Short description of the company, your responsibilities, and top level results. Unique info compared to the skills above and the other companies. No repetition! Should not be more than 2-3 lines of description per company.

Kolider Partners Healdsburg, CA
Title, (April 2007 to June 2009)
• Same

Include all companies since graduation – less and less description the older the companies get

EDUCATION

Bachelor of Liberal Studies in Business Administration May 2006
UNIVERSITY OF MARY WASHINGTON, Fredericksburg, Virginia

INTERVIEWING SKILLS

EXCELLING AT YOUR INTERVIEW – Success Opportunities

PREPARE FOR YOUR INTERVIEW:
If you have the opportunity, develop skills in practice interviews. Practicing will add to your self-confidence and reduce the normal anxieties associated with interviewing with a prospective employer. Be prepared to answer any of the typical interview questions used in job interviews. A list of some of the common interview questions follows and may be used for role-plays of practice interviews.

MANAGE STRESS AND PERSONAL ANXIETIES:
Be prepared to deal with the stress inherent in interviewing for jobs. Interviews often evoke fear of failure and interpersonal insecurities that may interfere with your achieving your best impression. Use self-assessment strategies to identify any problem areas and design self-management strategies to reduce your personal stress and interviewing pressures.

DRESS FOR SUCCESS:
Research indicates the first impression is visual and therefore how you dress and groom yourself has a lasting impression on the interviewer. It is important to dress as you imagine the interviewer would like you to dress to maximize your positive first impression.

ARRIVE EARLY:
Reduce your stress by leaving extra time to make sure you can find the agency and office of the interviewer by the time of your appointment. Demonstrate that you are conscientious, reliable, motivated and committed by arriving early and using the extra time to focus your energies on your prospective interview.

GREET WITH A FIRM HANDSHAKE AND A SMILE
It is important to project a friendly, warm personality that is genuinely interested in meeting and greeting the interviewer. Be sure to be assertive and shake the person's hand as you greet them, making warm eye contact. Be friendly and courteous and let them know that you are appreciative of their time and willingness to interview you for the position.

SHOW ENTHUSIASM, INTEREST AND KNOWLEDGE
Nothing is as contagious and impressive as pure enthusiasm. Having a positive attitude creates a lasting positive impression and is essential for building a positive relationship with the interviewer. Show interest not only in the potential service-learning position but also in the interviewer. Everyone likes someone who is genuinely interested in them and makes them feel important. Ask questions that show you care about the company and the interviewer and that you want to make a positive difference through your work.

EMPHASIZE PERSONAL STRENGTHS AND POTENTIAL CONTRIBUTIONS
Be sure to engage in a two-way conversation that allows you to find out what the interviewer is looking for and highlight the ways in which you fit their description.

REEMPHASIZE YOUR INTEREST, COMMITMENT AND AFTER-INTERVIEW PLANS
Be sure to reaffirm your commitment as you complete the interview and to thank them for their time. Follow-up with a thank-you letter and phone call to reaffirm your commitment.

COMMON INTERVIEW QUESTIONS

1. What are your strengths and weaknesses?
2. What personal skills or talents do you offer or bring to this position?
3. What are your career goals? How might this position help you achieve your career goals?
4. What are your personal goals and ways you might want to make a difference in the world? How does this relate to the potential position or job opportunity?
5. Why did you choose to apply at this organization or for this particular job position?
6. What work or volunteer experience has been most important to you and why?
7. What factors did you consider in choosing your major?
8. Who or what has been the greatest influence in your choice of a career or major?
9. What is your GPA? Does it reflect your ability and personal dedication to your future career?
10. What interests or concerns you about the position, the company or the agency?
11. Tell me about yourself.
12. Describe your leadership style.
13. Describe any leadership roles or projects you have played a leadership role in developing.
14. What are the qualities of a good team-player? What qualities do you possess and offer a team?
15. Give examples how your strengths and weaknesses might affect your performance in this position you are interviewing for now.
16. Give an example of a problem you have solved and what skills you demonstrated in solving the problem. Or what is your method for resolving conflict? What is your conflict-management style?
17. What idea have you developed and implemented that was particularly creative or innovative?
18. How do you motivate people? What motivates you?
19. What were your extracurricular activities? Why did you choose these activities and what do you gain or learn from your involvement?
20. What has been a great challenge in your life? How have you dealt with it or overcome the obstacles?
21. What characteristics do you think are important for this position?
22. What can you contribute to the agency or the clients?
23. How are you conducting your job search and how will you make a decision?
24. How would your friends describe you? (alternatives: your professors, your parents, your last employer)
25. What else should I know about you?

Close Friends Who Are Well Connected	Neighborhood Friends	Prior Neighborhood Friends	College and High School Friends	Influential Facebook and LinkedIn Connections
Parents, Friends and Connections of Close Friends	Aunts, Uncles, Cousins & Other Relatives	Prior supervisors, and supervisors of prior supervisors	Co-workers, Prior Coworkers, Clients, Prior-Clients	People Through Associations: sports teams, church, clubs

Pre-Networking Meeting Checklist

- [ ] BEFORE MEETING DAY: Research the company and industry that you will be talking about
- [ ] Schedule meeting for at least 45 minutes
- [ ] Select a clean and professional location - coffee shop or?
- [ ] Dress professionally to make a good impression, even if you know this person well
- [ ] Arrive 15 minutes early in case your guest is early as well, and to ensure you are not late
- [ ] Make sure to pay for the coffee
- [ ] Open conversation with pleasantries, how family is doing, etc.
- [ ] Practice good eye contact and posture
- [ ] Transition to your job search, and be very specific about what kind of job you are looking for
- [ ] First seek advice, and hint occaisionally that you need some referrals
- [ ] If by the end of the conversation no introductions have been offered, you can gently ask
- [ ] Make sure to thank them generously when they do offer somebody for you to meet
- [ ] Make sure to follow up with a thank-you note withing 24 hours
- [ ] Thank them again for the introduction after you have met with that person

Acknowledgements

Over the years many friends have contributed to my understanding of how this industry works and several friends who have helped move me to get this book written. For their patience and assistance helping me with the industry, a warm thanks to John and JW Ferneborg, John Bronson, Vito Bialla, Jim Mead, Steve O'Deegan, Rusty Rueff and Laura Putnam. For assistance mentoring me through the process of hiring and managing people, thanks to John Riccitiello, Melinda Gates, Peter Kendall, Carl Gulledge, Bill Morrissey, and Janet Brady. and for patience and enthusiasm with my requests for assistance with the book editing and content, Michael Collopy, Michael Grimes, Alexander Tamas, Dave Weir, Steve Bard, Randy Martin, and Scott Jessup. And a big thanks to mentors not already listed, Mark Effle, Betty and Rick Farrell, and Edward Tauber. And to my wife Lori, and daughters Noelle and Christina, thanks for unlimited patience with my long hours and eccentricities, your support makes everything possible.

Suggested Reading

In my opinion, Daniel Pink is the most important author for all information pertaining to careers. He has yet to release a job-finding book, but I will be first on his list if he does. I recommend each of his books as I find his perspectives not only insightful, but each book has a flavor completely unique from the other.

The Adventures of Johnny Bunko, by Daniel Pink
A quick read with a unique approach at conveying six important lessons for careers. At least one of these six points will be an important insight for you.

A Whole New Mind, by Daniel Pink
A peek into the future of work and the mindset for success in the future.

Drive, by Daniel Pink
A fun and insightful look at personal motivation

Other suggested books:

Never Eat Alone, by Keith Ferrazzi (the first 80 pages)

The Social Animal, by David Brooks

Outliers, by Malcolm Gladwell

Awaken the Giant Within, by Anthony Robbins

Suggested Viewing

From Ted.com, two videos I think everyone should see, particularly when conducting a job search:

How to live before you die, Steve Jobs

The power of vulnerability, Brené Brown: